A
SELF-SUFFICIENT
LARDER

To Bean and Armo and all those
who strive for a saner future.

OPTIMA

A
SELF-SUFFICIENT
LARDER

MIKE FOXWELL

ILLUSTRATED BY JANE O'NEILL

An OPTIMA book

© Mike Foxwell 1988

First published in 1988 by
Macdonald Optima, a division of
Macdonald & Co. (Publishers) Ltd

A Pergamon Press plc company

British Library Cataloguing in Publication Data

Foxwell, Mike
  A Self-sufficient larder.
  1. Food : Dishes using natural food – Recipes
  I. Title
  641.5′637

  ISBN 0-356-14860-2

Macdonald & Co. (Publishers) Ltd
3rd Floor
Greater London House
Hampstead Road
London NW1 7QX

Printed and bound in Great Britain by
The Guernsey Press Co. Ltd,
Guernsey, Channel Islands

CONTENTS

Acknowledgements

My grateful thanks are due to my mother, who tested many of the recipes, and also to my father, for carefully testing the wine recipes and helping me to prepare the photographs which were the basis for the illustrations. Thanks also to Dean Braithwaite, who not only tried out the recipes but patiently read the manuscript and offered many helpful suggestions as well. Any errors which remain are entirely my own responsibility. I would also like to acknowledge the patient and painstaking efforts of Jane O'Neill, who spent many hours drawing and redrawing the illustrations. Finally, I would like to offer my deepest thanks to Andy Armitage, without whose help and encouragement this book would never have been written.

INTRODUCTION

This book is a practical guide to producing wholesome foods at home for yourself. Home-produced food has an undeniable rustic appeal, but there are more important reasons for considering it as an alternative to simply buying your provisions from the local supermarket. If you make your own foods, whole vistas of choice open up to you, because *you* are in control of the finished product – be it sausages or beer.

Real choice is something sadly lacking in the modern supermarket, which no longer caters for regional variation in our diet. Instead of stocking once-famous local cheeses, supermarket shelves nowadays are filled with bland, nondescript cheeses that were made in some huge factory a hundred miles away. But things weren't always this way: once upon a time, cheeses were made on local farms, hams and bacon were cured by small family firms that really cared about the quality of their meats, and beer was brewed by a host of local breweries. In Coventry, where I live, there were once as many as 68 brewers! Sadly, the last brewery in Coventry closed more than 60 years ago, a tale that typifies the fate of so much of our once locally produced food. Now we have huge, profit-oriented food factories churning out vast quantities of dull, amorphous, low-grade products that sell in equally dull and amorphous supermarkets up and down the country. Making your own foods is an excellent way of turning the clock back to a saner age.

THE BANE OF CENTRALIZATION

The chief factor in the demise of locally produced food is centralization: Once, food was produced in small, locally owned factories dotted about the country, but now most of it is turned out by massive industrial plants owned by a handful of companies. As a consequence of this centralization, the general quality of our food is much poorer. The reason for this is not difficult to understand: as soon as big businesses become involved in food production, economy takes precedence over quality, and as any business man or woman will tell you, to increase profits you have to cut costs. For the food industry, an obvious way to cut costs is to use cheaper, lower-quality raw ingredients. Pork pies are an example; at one time, only meat would have been used to fill a pork pie, whereas nowadays the typical supermarket pork pie is quite likely to contain such repulsive animal scraps as rectums, spinal cords and testicles, things which would once have been consigned to the knacker's yard. Of course, it is the technology that these companies can so readily afford that enables them to make use of these ingredients; a small, traditional pie-maker could never have concealed the presence of such rubbish in his pies.

Another way the food processors achieve 'economies of scale' is by cutting down on the range of foods they produce. 'But ah, wait a minute!', says the food industry. 'Take a look at any supermarket and see the vast range of different foods we stock its shelves with – the consumer has never had greater choice!' Yes, do take a look at the foods on sale at your local supermarket; take a really close look at the lists of ingredients. What you will find is that a surprising number of foods that *appear* from the advertising on the packets to be quite different from each other, are made of the same basic ingredients: modified starch, fats, sugar (or some artificial sweetener), salt and a dazzling array of chemical additives. Compare the ingredients of an instant packet soup with those of a dessert mix, and you will be hard pressed to find much difference. The vision of choice is a mere illusion; sweep away these novel foods – really nothing more than chemical cocktails – and the shelves would look bare indeed.

THE ROLE OF ADDITIVES

What is the secret of the nefarious alchemy used by the food industry to convert such base things as starch and fat into 'foods' as diverse in appearance as soup and instant desserts? Added colourings and flavourings hold the key. With the aid of these things the industry can deceive us into believing that what we are buying and eating is more wholesome and nutritious than it actually is. The truth is that about 90 per cent of the additives in our food are colourings, flavourings and texture modifiers used purely cosmetically to hide the true nature of the product. The use of these cosmetic additives amounts to nothing less than legalized fraud. Interestingly, medieval food legislation was very strict, controlling the composition of many foods through instruments such as Assize of bread and ale. Since then, of course, we have progressed to such an extent that the food industry can put more or less what chemical adulterants it likes into our food with the total complicity of the law.

So widespread is the use of additives in our food that even on a conservative estimate, anyone on a typical British diet consumes about 3.5Kg (8lb) of these chemicals every year – equivalent to about 16 aspirin-sized tablets a day! Worse than that, many of these chemicals don't even have to be declared on the packet. Flavourings in particular don't have to be mentioned by name; they can all go quite legally by the generic term 'flavouring' only. It has been estimated that something like 6,000 different flavourings are used in our food, and apart from the food industry, only the government knows what they are. Apparently we don't have a right to know, since the government have promised the food industry that they'll keep it to themselves. The simple truth is that there are *no regulations whatever* controlling the use of flavourings, and the food industry can use whatever flavouring chemicals in whatever quantities it likes, all in total secrecy and with total impunity.

The use of colourings and flavourings may amount to legalized fraud, but surely the use of preservatives is rather more respectable? After all, aren't preservatives used to stop food going bad and prevent us all going down with food poisoning? But even though the use of preservatives may seem relatively straightforward and innocuous, all is not what it might seem. Under the government food regulations, a preservative is defined as 'Any substance which is capable of inhibiting, retarding or arresting the growth of micro-organisms or any deterioration of food due to micro-organisms or of masking the evidence of any such deterioration'. What this means is that the industry can quite legally add chemicals to our food to hide the fact that their products are stale or even decomposing!

ARE ADDITIVES SAFE?

By now it should be clear that the use of the vast majority of additives is a kind of legalized deception, but what effect do they have on those of us who eat them? Are additives really safe? It is this facet of the additives question that has received the widest public airing in recent years. It would be quite reasonable to assume – as most people do – that the additives that go into our food have been tested by experts and found to be safe, but if you believed that you'd be wrong. Flavourings are the obvious example: there are no regulations at all governing the use of these substances, and they can be used entirely without restriction, and without any proof whatsoever that they are safe. Colourings provide other examples: in 1979 the Ministry of Agriculture's Food Additives and Contaminants Committee (FACC) considered that insufficient data was available on the colouring Patent Blue V (E131) for them to assess whether or not it was safe. In spite of this, Patent Blue still remained in use.

Even when real doubts about the safety of additives are raised, nothing is done. Take for instance the case of Brown FK, a brown colouring used, among other things, to dye kippers to make them appear smoked. In 1978 a joint United Nations and World Health Organization committee of experts stated that Brown FK is harmful to the heart and causes liver damage in mice and genetic damage to bacteria. In spite of these grave doubts about its safety, it was not banned. Another example is supplied by the various nitrates and nitrites used in everything from cheese to meat pastes – and, of course, in cured meats, to give them their attractive, rosy hue. These additives form highly carcinogenic (cancer-causing) substances called nitrosamines, both in the foods that contain them and in our stomachs when they are eaten. Even the FACC recognized the dangers of these unnecessary additives as long ago as 1978 when it pronounced that their use in food should be discontinued as soon as possible. Ten years later they are still being used.

DOES 'NATURAL' = 'SAFE'?

Another twist to the additives story is the increasing use of natural flavourings and colourings. The food industry has started using natural alternatives to synthetic dyes and flavours because the public has, over the last few years, become sensitized to the potential hazards of food additives. Despite the growing public awareness about food and diet in general, and additives in particular, most people still believe that anything 'natural' will be safe to eat. Nothing could be further from the truth: many natural colourings such as the caramels and turmeric are also highly suspect. The latter has been found to cause genetic damage to bacteria, and some forms of caramel have been found to cause blood disorders in laboratory animals. We shouldn't be at all surprised that this is so – after all, arsenic is natural too.

HOW ADDITIVES ARE TESTED

Broadly speaking, there are three ways to test the safety of an additive: you can try it out on people, you can test it on laboratory animals, or you can feed it to bacteria or tissue cultures. The only real way to be sure whether an additive is safe or not is to try it out on people. This, of course, would be morally unacceptable – although to judge from the attitude of successive governments to controlling the use of suspect additives, you could argue that the general public is being experimented on now. Suppose that an additive already in use was doing harm to the people who consumed it; the chances are that you would only spot this if 10 to 15 per cent of the population was affected, and only if the effects were of an acute, short-term nature such as headaches or diarrhoea. Chronic long-term consequences like cancer would not be easy to detect by these methods, so it is quite possible that additives now in use could produce cancers and similar diseases in people who consumed them for long periods of time – say forty years or so – even if in short-term laboratory studies they seemed safe.

More usually, additives are tried out on laboratory animals or bacteria. Whether the results of tests on, say, rats have any demonstrable implications for human beings is highly debatable, and there certainly are substances which are carcinogenic to humans but harmless to laboratory animals, and vice versa. The thalidomide tragedy is an extremely ominous warning of the risks the so-called 'science' of toxicology is taking with our health and well-being. This drug, pronounced safe by standard toxicological methods, turned out to be far more dangerous to human beings than to the laboratory animals it was tested on.

Toxicology owes more to politics than it does to science; indeed, it seems to have no scientific foundation at all.

To illustrate this point let me describe how a fictitious additive, which I shall call Ultra-Violet 3, would probably be safety-tested. The test is conducted by feeding various doses of Ultra-Violet 3 to some laboratory rats. What is found after feeding the rats this additive for a few months is that some of them develop cancers. On closer inspection it turns out that there is a high incidence of cancer among those rats given doses above a certain level, say level x. Note that the only thing this experiment has proved is that Ultra-Violet 3 is carcinogenic to rats. What the scientists deduce, erroneously, from this result, is that Ultra-Violet 3 does not cause cancer in rats at doses *below* x, an utterly invalid assumption, since they have fed the additive to the rats for only a few months. Had they continued the experiment for several years, they might well have discovered that doses lower than x also produced cancers. In short, there is no scientific basis to the deduction that low doses of Ultra-Violet 3 are safe for rats in the long term. Having 'proved' that Ultra-Violet 3 is safe for rats in small doses, they now have the problem of extrapolating their 'result' to human beings. What they do next defies belief: they arbitrarily assume that a dose one hundredth of that which produced no effect in the rats is safe for humans! What grounds are there for this assumption, especially in view of the fact that in all probability the effects of Ultra-Violet 3 on humans have never been studied? The answer is quite simple: there is no scientific basis whatever for this assumption either, and in cases where the test results look less clear-cut, this 'fiddle factor' can be increased by 10 or 20 times, no doubt to calm the nerves of the legislators.

The final flaw in the testing of our additive is that no account whatever is taken of the so-called 'cocktail effect', whereby when additives are consumed in combinations, as in the real world they always are, their effects can be more serious than if they were consumed singly. Because of the enormous number of different additives used in our food, the number of possible combinations would be truly astronomical, and would defy all attempts at analysis. For example, a typical processed food is likely to contain on average between four and seven different additives. Since there are around 6,000 different food additives in general use, the total number of combinations of four additives at a time is more than 10^{15}. This means that to determine whether each possible combination is safe or not would require something of the order of 10^{15} separate studies. Even if one study were completed every second this would still take more than forty million years!! Real studies take years to complete, not seconds, and even if all the studies could be done, they would still not take account of the endless variations in the quantity of additives put into food, nor would they take any account of the fact that most people consume not just four different additives a day but dozens. Here, then, founders all hope of ever proving additives truly safe.

'COOKING THE BOOKS'

Even when safety studies are done on food additives, very often the work is undertaken by the same company that seeks to gain government approval for the additive. In sharp contrast with the practice in many other countries, our government doesn't commission independent investigations into additives and won't even declare what criteria (if any) it uses to determine whether or not a given additive is safe. Even when data is submitted to the various government committees, the whole thing is shrouded in secrecy, since both the machinations of the committees and the raw data on which they base their judgements are kept from the public by the Official Secrets Act.

This secrecy has profound implications, since studies are not always performed impartially, and sometimes the results are deliberately distorted and manipulated – or simply faked, as happened with the American company Industrial Bio-Test. IBT were commissioned to undertake toxicological studies, and were at one time responsible for nearly a third of all the studies performed worldwide. In 1976 it slowly became apparent that the company had, over the years, systematically faked hundreds of test results. These revelations led eventually to the trial and conviction of senior IBT employees in 1983 and the closing down of the company. The question remains however of how many dangerous additives have been passed as safe by our government (and others) on bogus data provided by IBT. As long as the operations of the various regulatory bodies remain an Official Secret we shall never know. It would be naively optimistic to believe that the IBT case was an isolated incident.

THE ALTERNATIVES

In view of all this uncertainty about additives, the only sensible thing to do is reduce our intake of *all* additives. Because of the close association of governments and the food industry, it seems somewhat optimistic to expect additives to be more effectively controlled, let alone outlawed, in the foreseeable future. The only option then, in the short term at least, is either to buy additive-free food or else shoulder a greater responsibility ourselves for what we eat. Whilst it is possible to buy certain additive-free foods, by no means is this *always* possible; for example, try finding bacon or ham made without nitrates or nitrites. Of course, supermarket foods contain other dubious ingredients in addition to the additives – usually lots of salt, fats and sugar too. Once again, you can sometimes avoid these things, but very often salt-, sugar- and additive-free equivalents are far more expensive than ordinary brands. Few of us can afford this, and even if we could, there is a far more restricted choice of these healthier foods.

For most of us, the only realistic alternative if we really care about what we eat, is to start making our own foods. This is not as daunting or as difficult as it may sound, and this book gives instructions, which I hope are both clear and simple, for making a wide range of the foods most of us consume in considerable amounts. To make them successfully and efficiently requires little or no special equipment, and what items of equipment you may have to buy are usually quite inexpensive. Making your own foods isn't as time-consuming as you perhaps might expect, either; for example, sausages and burgers can be made in large quantities that will last you for months, and simply frozen until needed. Patés too can be made in bulk, and will provide tasty meals for weeks or months to come; and for only a couple of hours' work a week, you can keep your family supplied with delicious, oven-fresh wholemeal bread.

At the end of the book there is a chapter on growing herbs without the use of dangerous pesticides and artificial fertilizers. Herbs truly are the cook's best ally; they provide character and flavour to even the most mundane dishes, and are used extensively in the recipes throughout this book. Finally, there is a further information section listing the names and addresses of specialist suppliers who can provide any of the more unusual bits and pieces that your local shops may not stock.

Throughout the book I have endeavoured to give as much information as possible about the whys and wherefores of producing your own foods, so that you will know *why* you are doing things, rather than just blindly following endless lists of recipes. Armed with this information you will be better equipped to adapt recipes to suit your own particular likes and needs, and you will be able to make fuller use of recipes in other books which give the reader none of the essential background to the processes involved. All the recipes contained in this book are well tried and trusted, and are the result of much experimentation over the last twelve years. However, should you encounter problems for any reason, I should be pleased to advise you personally if you care to write to me via the publisher, enclosing a stamped addressed envelope.

1.
BREAD

Making your own bread is undoubtedly one of the most
rewarding of all the kitchen crafts. But this aside, why
bother making your own? Well, needless to say, homemade
bread tastes a whole lot better than what you've been buying
up to now, but there is another important reason: if you
make it yourself, you know what you're getting.

It was only as recently as September 1984 that regulations
(Bread and Flour Regulations 1984, SI No 1304, HMSO)
were brought into force which required bakers to declare in
the list of ingredients a whole range of additives called 'flour
improvers' which they freely add to our daily bread.
Although the addition of flour *improvers* might seem quite a
laudable practice, the term improver is just another one of
those deceptive euphemisms beloved of the food industry. In
plain English, a flour improver is a bleach, just like the stuff
you clean the toilet with. As you might expect, bleaches are
not good things to eat; in fact they are poisonous. Not only
are they poisonous in themselves, but they also destroy the
vitamin E in the flour, and may harm other nutritious
elements as well. Why then are these dangerous chemicals
used at all? Predictably, they are used to help the baker
make a bigger profit, since flour treated with these
improvers makes a stronger and more resilient dough which
can hold more water and gas, so making lighter, more
profitable loaves. At one time this effect was achieved
naturally, by simply storing the flour for a few weeks before
use, but like all natural processes, ageing the flour in this
way doesn't produce the even, consistent result given by
modern high-tech bread-making techniques. Even so, in
many countries – France and Belgium, for instance – the use

of flour improvers is quite rightly banned, on the grounds that these chemicals are both dangerous and unnecessary. Nonetheless it would seem that these countries are still able to produce perfectly saleable bread.

Although the regulations requiring flour improvers to be declared officially came into force in September 1984, a clever piece of wording effectively let the bread industry off the hook until July 1986, a measure of how seriously the Ministry of Agriculture is concerned about the health and well-being of the British public. Another little loop-hole left by the Ministry allows the use of some types of improver without the need to declare their presence on the label at all. You will remember I pointed out earlier than another name for 'improver' is 'bleach'; and sure enough, improvers do bleach white flour whiter than white. Well, provided the only reason you include an improver is to bleach the flour rather than improve it – if you see what I mean – then that 'improver' isn't an improver, it's a bleach, and so doesn't have to be declared! One very common improver which neatly slips through this loop-hole, and which a government committee advised should be banned as long ago as 1927, is benzoyl peroxide. Doubtless there are others.

WHITE OR BROWN?

While it is certainly true that far more additives are permitted in white bread than in wholemeal – including some of the most controversial, such as chlorine dioxide, potassium bromate and other bleaches – it is equally true that wholemeal bread, while having nowt taken out, usually has plenty put in.

White bread has other nutritional defects as well – like having only 68 per cent of the iron found in wholemeal bread, or only 69 per cent of the vitamin B1, or less than a third of the fibre content, to name but three. This is hardly surprising, since the most nourishing parts of the wheat have been removed in the milling and refining process. What is left is so poor nutritionally, that even the legislators insist that it is enriched with iron and two B vitamins. (Incidentally, the figures given earlier refer to white bread made with so-called *enriched* flour!) To view human health solely in terms of a handful of measurable constituents of this food or that is recklessly naive, as year by year more and more previously unsuspected nutritive components of the food we eat are found to be vital to our good health. The truth is slowly emerging that we need the *whole* of our food to attain and maintain full health, and that means, in this instance, wholemeal bread.

Note that I say *wholemeal* and not just brown; there is a very great distinction. Brown bread is simply white bread with a bit of bran put back in; even with this added bran, it still has less than two thirds the fibre content of real wholemeal bread. And just to make you think you're getting something rather different and more wholesome than you actually are, this type of bread is often dyed brown with caramel. Many people, including quite often the very people who are selling it, think that the term brown and wholemeal are synonymous and interchangeable – they definitely are not, so if you do have to buy your bread from time to time, beware.

WHOLEMEAL BREAD

Wholemeal bread has to be made with 100 per cent of the wheat grain, but can still have up to 30 different additives as well, including, would you believe, caramel. This is something the bakers try to play down with their cleverly nostalgic advertising campaigns that appeal to our sepia-tinted sense of wholesomeness and (ironically) honesty.

Additives aside, I can quite truthfully say that I have never tasted commercially made wholemeal bread that tastes a tenth as good as the bread I make myself. Although I have made white bread occasionally in the past, I do think it's a shame to waste time on something that is nutritionally sub-standard to start with, when for no extra trouble you can have something which is not only much tastier, but healthier eating to boot. Accordingly, the recipes I have given below are for good old wholemeal – and I make no apologies for it!

MAKING WHOLEMEAL BREAD

There is absolutely no excuse for spending all day making bread by long-winded 'traditional' methods when there are quick methods which make truly superb bread in half the time. The two recipes below are both quick to do, but the second one is extremely fast, and with a little practice you should be able to turn your bread out in less than three hours from start to finish. To be honest, I think the first recipe has the edge as far as flavour and fineness of texture is concerned, but there's not much in it – try both and see for yourself!

A WORD ABOUT INGREDIENTS

Yeast, Flour and Ovens

Many people have told me in quite uncompromising terms that they cannot make bread. No matter what recipe they use it always turns out a disaster. Usually they mean it's too dense and hard, or else that it is too soft and doughy. Very often these calamities are caused by one of three faults. The first, and most common, is that people tend to follow recipes slavishly, like robots in a car factory. This might be fine for cars, but it certainly won't do for bread. The trouble is that the major ingredient of bread – flour – is so very variable, and never more so than in the case of wholemeal. This variability of, for instance, fineness and moisture content – and of goodness knows what else besides – makes a terrific difference to the amount of flour you should use to get a dough of a given consistency. Consequently, recipe slaves can easily end up with a dough that is either too wet or too dry, and this has a profound effect on the quality of the finished bread. What you should do instead is to start with a wet dough and add flour to it in *whatever amounts necessary* until the 'feel' of the dough is right. Don't worry, this isn't at all difficult! After you have made bread a few times, you will know instinctively when the dough feels right. Preparing your dough in this way is in sharp contrast to unthinkingly combining carefully measured amounts of water and flour in the way dictated by most recipes, and once you have mastered the technique you will be able to make perfect bread every time, whatever type or brand of flour you use.

Care with the Yeast

The second most common mistake is not taking due care with the yeast. Yeast works by fermenting sugars in the dough into carbon dioxide, which lodges in the bread as little bubbles – as a result, the bread rises. You must take care not to expose the yeast to excessive temperatures or you will kill it. I do mean *kill*, because yeast is actually a microscopic plant that likes to grow in sugary solutions at a temperature of around 27°C (80°F). Temperatures much above 32°C (90°F) will harm it, so if you are not that proficient at judging temperatures by touch alone, buy a thermometer. Freshness is the other thing to watch for. If you are using fresh yeast – and this is the best thing to do – be sure to go to a shop that sells a fair amount of it, or there is a danger it might be stale. You can tell if your yeast is stale by sniffing it and/or tasting a bit: if it smells or tastes at all acrid or 'strong' then it is stale and probably useless, although if it's all you've got, or you're not sure, you can test it first before you risk wasting your flour – see first recipe. If you can't get fresh yeast, dried will do; just use half the amount. You can do the same test to check its freshness. Fresh yeast will keep perfectly well in a refrigerator for a week, or can even be stored in a deep freeze, where it will keep well for a month to six weeks. Dried yeast will keep for months and months, provided it is kept in an airtight container in a cool, dry place.

Flour
The best sort of flour to use is made from organically grown wheat. You can either mill it yourself, as I do, or buy it from virtually any good wholefood shop. Take no notice of anyone who tries to tell you that you can only make bread with special 'strong' flour. I remember being told at great length by a cookery adviser that is was quite impossible to make bread with flour from wheat that isn't 'strong' enough (that is, doesn't have enough gluten in it – gluten enables the dough to hold bubbles of air and so allows bread to rise). She was not at all impressed when I told her I had been doing just that for years!

Ovens
The third common mistake is not to preheat the oven for long enough, or else to have the temperature set too low. If the oven is not really hot – about 230°C (450°F), gas mark 8 – not only will the bread not cook right through and be doughy in the middle, but you are also likely to find great holes in it caused by the agglomeration of tiny gas bubbles because the dough hasn't been set quickly enough to capture them.

Salt and Sugar
To my mind, or should I say palate, bread made without salt

has no taste at all, but no doubt many would disagree. Salt is in no sense an essential ingredient of bread, and can be safely omitted if you wish. If you do decide to use it, then buy good quality rock salt which is less likely to contain harmful contaminants, since it isn't made by evaporating present day highly polluted sea water. Obviously, the evaporation process extracts not only the salt from the water, but goodness-knows-what pollutants there are in it as well!

Sugar and honey, at least in the amounts suggested in the recipes below, serve only as a food for the yeast, and not as sweetener. Since wheat flour naturally contains something like 2.5 per cent of fermentable sugars which will feed the yeast anyway, you can omit the honey (or sugar) if you wish; but remember, if you do, your bread may take longer to rise.

RECIPES

Wholemeal bread (quick recipe)

1.125–1.35 kg (2½–3lb) wholemeal flour
750ml (1¼pts) warm water (80°F)
30g (1oz) fresh yeast or 15g (½oz) dried
2 rounded teaspoon sugar or honey
4 teaspoon salt

Dissolve the sugar or honey in the warm water, and then crumble the fresh yeast into it; if you are using dried yeast, just sprinkle this into the warm water. Take great care the water isn't too hot or you will kill the yeast. Leave until it starts to froth; this should take about five to ten minutes. If after half an hour it hasn't frothed, there is something wrong with the yeast and you will have to postpone breadmaking until you can get some more.

Assuming all is well with the yeast, put about 675g (1½lb) of the flour into a large bowl, sprinkle on the salt and mix well with your fingers. When making bread, it is always a good idea – though by no means essential – to warm both the flour and the bowl beforehand by standing them in a warm room, or near your stove, the night before. An airing cupboard would do just as well.

When frothy, pour the yeasty liquid onto the flour and stir well with a wooden spoon. You should add more flour, stirring well between additions, until the mixture becomes a

Knead the dough by alternately pushing it away from you (stretching it as much as possible), then pulling it back towards you, rolling it up slightly in the process. After kneading, the dough should look rather like a Swiss Roll.

stiff paste. Now cover the bowl with a damp cloth to prevent the paste drying out, and stand in a warm place. It should be left to ferment for at least an hour, or even overnight. The longer you leave it, the more flavour the bread will have, but don't leave it longer than overnight, or the yeast will use up all the sugar and the bread won't rise properly in the tins. This fermentation process not only improves the flavour of the bread, it also helps to activate the gluten in the flour, enabling the bread to hold more bubbles of carbon dioxide and making it lighter. If you have ever wondered why most commercial bread is so lacking in flavour, it is partly because this fermentation stage is completely omitted by 'high-tech' bakers. In such abominations as the Chorleywood Process, by which the vast majority of bread is now made, they use additives and mechanical agitation instead of allowing the dough to ferment properly.

At the end of the fermentation period, you should stir the paste well, and then mix in enough of the remaining flour to form a stiff dough. At this point, turn the dough out onto a floured working surface and begin kneading it. You can knead the bread any way you like – there are no rules. Having said that, I find the best way to do it is to roll the dough up towards you, Swiss roll fashion, stretching it as much as you can in the process. Then, when it's fully rolled up that way, turn it through 90 degrees and repeat the exercise, then turn it and knead again and so on. You will probably find the dough sticks to your hands in the early stages, so whenever it does, sprinkle on more flour and knead it in. When the dough becomes dry and springy, don't add any more flour, but continue kneading for a further ten minutes or so. The kneading helps develop the gluten further, and also distributes it throughout the dough, so improving the final texture of the bread. It is impossible to over-knead the dough, so relax and enjoy what is a very soothing exercise!

When you decide the dough has had enough kneading, grease your bread tins well and divide it up into pieces big enough to fill your tins to between a third and a half full, pushing the dough well into the corners with your knuckles. Be sure not to overfill the tins or there won't be enough room for the dough to rise and your bread will be heavy and close-textured. Once you have put the dough in the tins, cover with a damp cloth and leave in a warm place for the dough to rise. This recipe should make enough dough to half fill two 1kg (2lb) tins with maybe a little over. Any surplus dough can be used to make rolls: form it into balls, place on a greased baking sheet, cover with a damp cloth and leave to rise.

As soon as the dough has risen above the tops of the tins, take the cloth off and transfer them gently to a high shelf of your oven which should have been thoroughly preheated to 230°C (450°F), gas mark 8. The loaves should take about 30–40 minutes to cook, depending on your oven. To test whether they are cooked, simply turn them out of their tins and tap the bottoms. If the bottoms feel firm and sound hollow, they are cooked. If not, return them to the tins and bake them for a little longer. When cooked, turn the bread out and either stand the loaves on a cooling rack or across the tops of the tins. (The rolls should be baked in a similar way once they have doubled in size, but don't cook them as long – 20 to 30 minutes is about right.)

If you want crustier loaves, brush the tops with milk or beaten egg before baking. If you like sesame or poppy seeds on the top, brush the loaves with milk or egg and sprinkle with seeds just before you put them in the oven. Alternatively, roll the dough in the seeds before filling the tins.

Wholemeal bread (very quick recipe)

This recipe is even quicker than the previous one, and doesn't require any kneading at all! The ingredients are exactly as for the recipe above.

Dissolve the sugar or honey in the warm water, add the yeast and leave until frothy. Put 675g (1½lb) of the flour into a large bowl and add the salt, mixing well. When the liquid has frothed, pour into the bowl and stir well to incorporate all the flour to form a thick paste. Cover the bowl with a damp cloth and leave in a warm place to ferment for about 45 minutes.

Now add more flour, a little at a time, stirring well between additions until you have a nice firm dough that holds together in one lump. Divide the dough between two well-greased bread tins, no more than half filling them. Cover the tins with a damp cloth and leave to rise in a warm place. Any dough left over is best stiffened first with a little more flour and kneaded before being made into rolls, since the unstiffened dough is too soft to be baked without the support of a tin. When the dough reaches the tops of the tins, remove the cloth and bake exactly as before (see page 25) – except that bread made by this recipe will require longer cooking: 40–50 minutes is about right for loaves, and 30–40 minutes for rolls. As with the previous recipe, if you want a crustier loaf, glaze it with milk or egg just before you bake it, and if you like seeds on your bread, stick them on with egg or milk.

Variations

One of the real beauties of being your own baker is that you can vary your recipes to give extra variety to your bread. For example, try replacing up to a third of the wheat flour in the basic recipes with a different kind of flour: using a third rye flour, for instance, adds smoothness and bite but makes the texture coarser. If you use oatmeal, your bread will be denser and sweeter. Millet flour (if you can get it) makes the bread crumblier and gives a pleasant crunch to it. Maize flour (cornmeal) also makes the bread crumblier and adds sweetness.

Whichever flour, or combination of these special flours you try, ensure they don't account for more than a third of the total quantity of flour, or else your bread will tend to fall apart when you cut into it.

Delicious cheese bread

This is one of the tastiest variations of all. You can use
either of the basic recipes given above, but reduce the
amount of water used to 512ml (18fl oz), and add 340g (12oz)
of strong cheddar cheese to the paste before you leave it to
ferment; otherwise continue as directed in the basic recipes.

STORING BREAD

Never put your bread away in your bread bin until it is
completely cooled, or else it will grow mould and be quickly
ruined. Contrary to popular belief, storing bread in a
refrigerator does *not* prevent it from staling – in fact, it
accelerates it.

2.
CHUTNEYS, SAUCES AND KETCHUPS

One of the most striking things about the ordinary supermarket brands of chutney is their overpowering sweetness, and the same goes for sauces and ketchups as well. Just how much sugar is used in these commercially made preserves was brought home to me recently when I did a survey of a wide range of common supermarket brands. I was utterly astounded to find that the most abundant ingredient in some brands of chutney was sugar itself! This really is shocking when you consider the adverse effect excessive sugar consumption can have on health, and that it is in any case perfectly possible to make delicious chutneys without sugar at all! The food manufacturers know this as well; they sometimes choose to use artificial sweeteners in the form – most often – of saccharin, either instead of sugar or else to supplement it. This is hardly an improvement, as saccharin has a long and well-documented record of being toxic, and surely must be at least as dangerous as sugar.

Salt is the other ubiquitous ingredient in commercial chutneys and sauces. Out of twenty different types of chutney I found on the shelves of three national supermarkets, all of them contained salt. This too is amazing – I haven't used salt in my homemade preserves for years, and not one of my family has ever noticed its absence!

This almost universal use of sugar and salt is worrying for another reason, namely that these ingredients can mask the shortcomings of products with little in the way of legitimate ingredients – that is to say, fruit and vegetables. As well as an abundance of sugar and salt, the great majority of supermarket chutneys and sauces also contain modified starch. Modified starch is the food industry's favourite

thickening concoction, and is used in everything from dry
roast peanuts to packet dessert mixes. Although it sounds
fairly innocuous, modified starches are suspected carcinogens
and are consequently highly questionable additives which
should be avoided. When used in sauces, chutneys and the
like, modified starches serve to thicken up nauseating
concoctions of water, sugar, salt and other additives, and so
fool the purchaser into thinking there is a higher fruit or
vegetable content than there actually is.

GROWING YOUR OWN

If you have all but the smallest vegetable or fruit garden,
you will undoubtedly find yourself with gluts of produce
from time to time, especially in the Autumn. Making
chutneys and sauces is an ideal way of cashing in on your
embarrassment of riches. You could of course bottle or make
jam of surpluses of fruits (most vegetables are not acidic
enough to be preserved by these methods, and would taste
odd if acid were added), but if you have a real glut to get rid
of, then nothing swallows up large quantities of fruits and
vegetables like chutneys, sauces and ketchups. A quick
glance at the price labels of salt-, sugar- and additive-free
preserves in the health food shops will soon convince you
that making your own still makes good economic sense even
if you haven't got a garden and have to buy all the
ingredients. Even assuming average prices for the
ingredients, you ought to be able to make your own for less
than half the price, and if you take advantage of seasonal
gluts sold off at give-away prices, you can save even more
money.

CHOOSING INGREDIENTS

There are few hard and fast rules as far as making chutneys
and sauces is concerned. One thing to bear in mind, though,
is that the best preserves are usually made from a variety of
different types of fruits and/or vegetables, and not just a
single one. Even so, this isn't always the case; single fruit
chutneys can be very tasty if made well, and some single
fruit sauces – notably tomato – are tremendously popular.
But in general, the thing to bear in mind is that you should
aim to use ingredients that contrast well with each other.
For example, if you use cooking apples with red tomatoes,

the sharpness of the apples offsets the sweetness of the
tomatoes. With chutneys, you should also try to choose
ingredients which have contrasting colours and textures as
well, so as to add extra visual appeal to the end product. You
should bear in mind though that while some ingredients like
marrow and onion *do* hold their shape and colour well,
others such as apples and plums tend to turn into a
nondescript mush after a few hours' slow cooking.

ADAPTING RECIPES

The real beauty of chutneys and sauces is that you can adapt
recipes to suit the ingredients you have to hand or can buy
most cheaply. For instance, if a recipe calls for cucumber but
you have dozens of courgettes to use up, simply use the
courgettes instead. Similarly, you can substitute celery for
onions, or green tomatoes for red ones, or apples for pears
and so on. Always remember, though, that you must keep
the *relative* proportions of vinegar, fruit and vegetables, and
dried fruits about the same or the preserve may not keep. If
you are ever in any doubt about this, then use a little more
vinegar to be on the safe side.

You can use soft or over-ripe fruits and vegetables for
sauces and chutneys, but take great care you cut away any
bad or damaged parts before using them. During seasonal
gluts you will very often see market stalls selling off
damaged or over-ripe produce very cheaply. This sort of
produce is ideal for making chutneys and sauces so long as it
is basically sound, and you take the trouble to remove any
damaged or decayed parts before using it.

VINEGAR

Vinegar is the vital preservative in chutneys and sauces,
and without the (acetic) acid it supplies, the chutney or
sauce just wouldn't keep. Not surprisingly, then, the choice
of vinegar is of considerable importance, especially as it also
contributes to the overall flavour of the preserve. The
foremost consideration is its strength. It must be strong
enough – that is it must contain sufficient acetic acid – to
retard the growth of organisms that would otherwise spoil
the finished product. This is usually only stressed for
vinegars used for pickling, but is equally important for
chutney and sauce making, especially since the recipes in

this book do not contain salt, which in conventional recipes acts as a secondary preservative. The vinegar you use should have a minimum strength of about 5 per cent acetic acid. Ordinary bottled malt vinegars should meet this criterion; some even have their strength declared on the bottle, which is very reassuring. Malt vinegars that are sold on draught from bulk containers should be avoided, as they are often understrength and frequently contain dubious additives.

Flavour is the other important consideration when choosing your vinegar; for most chutneys and sauces, malt vinegar is the best choice and there are many different brands to choose from. Sadly, many malt vinegars have their colour artificially darkened by caramel. Caramel (E150), although sounding quite safe and homely, is a potentially harmful additive and has been linked with blood disorders and possibly cancer. Fortunately, caramel-free malt vinegars can be bought, and Sarsons is probably the most widely available brand. Another advantage of using caramel-free vinegar is that the flavour is likely to be superior to that of vinegars which are artificially dyed. This is because the use of caramel colouring suggests the manufacturer has cut back on the amount of (expensive) malt used to make the vinegar, and if this is the case, not only will the natural colour of the vinegar be poorer, the flavour will be as well.

Other vinegars useful in chutney and sauce making are those made from cider and wine. These vinegars, while being more expensive than malt vinegar, do have a finer flavour which is more suited to fancy or delicately flavoured chutneys and sauces – especially those that contain large amounts of fruit. Many people believe that cider and wine vinegars are very much stronger than malt vinegar, as I did until I did some tests on a wide range of cider and wine vinegars and found that there is often very little to choose, strength-wise, between a good malt vinegar and cider or wine vinegar. Even so, any good brand of cider or wine vinegar should contain at least 5 per cent acetic acid and will be perfectly suitable for chutney and sauce making. As with malt vinegar, cider and wine vinegars are also liable to have unnecessary chemicals added to them. This time it is sulphur dioxide in one form or another. Sulphur dioxide is a powerful irritant, and is especially dangerous to asthmatics. The appropriate 'E' numbers to avoid are E220 – E224, E226 and E227.

2. CHUTNEYS, SAUCES AND KETCHUPS

SPICES

Spices are an essential ingredient of chutneys and sauces, and give them their characteristically rich and aromatic flavour. When choosing spices for these preserves it is important to ensure that the flavour of the spice is in harmony with that of the basic ingredients. For example, if the recipe contains a large proportion of delicately flavoured fruits, then to make it hot and spicy with large amounts of mustard and peppers would probably be wholly inappropriate; save these for more piquant preserves. Rather, the choice here should be for more mellow, aromatic spices like cloves, nutmeg, cardamom, cinnamon, mace and so on. Even with this restriction there is still a tremendous amount of scope, and once you have gained a little experience you can experiment with various different blends of spice.

Using spice
There are two basic ways of using spices to flavour sauces and chutneys: you can use *whole* spice tied up in a little bag made from a square of muslin which you then drop into the preserve while it is cooking; or you can grind up the spices and simply dump them in with the rest of the ingredients. (If you use ground spices, always try to make sure they are *freshly* ground to give your chutneys the best possible flavour. If you haven't got a special spice mill, an ordinary manual or electric coffee grinder is perfectly suitable, but never try to grind dried root ginger, as this is very hard and may break your grinder. Alternatively, provided you've got plenty of patience, you can grind your spices with a mortar and pestle as the Indians do.) For chutney, I usually grind the spices, but if you are making a sauce where you want to retain a nice, bright, fresh colour, it is sometimes better to use whole spice, since ground spices tend to darken the colour. When using whole spices, make quite certain that the muslin bag is tied firmly closed; if the spices escape into the chutney you could never hope to strain them all out again, and the preserve could easily be ruined. Also, make sure the bag is large enough; the spices need to mingle freely with the liquid for their flavours and aroma to be fully extracted. And bear in mind that dried spices swell up as they absorb liquid, and this might enable them to squeeze out of the bag if it is too small. When spicing your preserve in this way, be

sure to attach the muslin bag securely to the handle of the pan with a piece of string, as this makes life easier when the time comes to fish it out.

EQUIPMENT FOR CHUTNEY AND SAUCE MAKING

You will need very little in the way of special equipment to make chutneys and sauces. Other than a sharp knife, or perhaps a mincer, to cut the ingredients up with, the main item you will need is a large pan to cook the preserve in. The best sort of pan to use is a wide, shallow one made of heavy-gauge stainless steel, but unfortunately they cost the earth, and I must admit I don't own one. What I use instead is a heavy-gauge aluminium equivalent. Aluminium pans are far from ideal, however, as the highly acidic chutney leaches aluminium from the pan. For most people this doesn't seem to cause problems – after all, many people cook food in aluminium pans every day – but there are people who have an aluminium intolerance (allergy), and for these people, eating foods that contain aluminium can result in various unpleasant effects such as itching and headaches.

There is one type of pan you must never under any circumstances use, and that is one made of copper or brass. The acid would leach out such large amounts of metal salts from these pans that the chutney or sauce would have a horrible metallic taste, and might well be poisonous too. Iron pans are also unsuitable unless they have an undamaged enamel lining.

You will also need a long-handled wooden spoon for stirring – the longer the handle the better, as in the final stages of cooking, the preserve will 'plop' out of the pan in hot dollops which will hurt if they land on you. I use a spoon with a 40cm (16 inch) long handle, which keeps my hands well clear of the wrath of my preserving pan – most of the time, at least! This type of spoon, often called a jam spoon, is available from good kitchen shops.

Finally, for chutney you will need some storage pots and a jam funnel and jug or ladle to bail the chutney out of the pan. The pots should be made of glass or pottery, and should ideally hold something like one or two pounds of chutney, depending on how quickly you are likely to get through it. Whatever sort of pots you use, they must have closely fitting vinegar proof lids. It is very important that the lids are an airtight fit or else the chutney will dry out in storage. Metal lids are fine provided they have an *intact* plastic coating inside. In my opinion, bottling jars with hermetic lids are the very best kind of pots to use. There are several different brands available, but I find the 'Kilner' range with plastic screw bands, made by Ravenhead Glass, are the best. As a rough guide, the 500g Kilner jars hold about 450g (1lb), and the 1 litre ones about 900g (2lb). If you cannot afford these, as I couldn't for many years, you can use empty jam and chutney jars instead. If you haven't got suitable screw tops for these jars you can use a special preserving film called Porosan instead – ordinary cellophane jam covers are *not* suitable, as the vinegar will rapidly evaporate through the cellophane, leaving your chutney dry, shrunken and inedible. Porosan is quite inexpensive to buy, and the manufacturers even claim it can be reused, although I have never found this to be the case. Good chemists or kitchen shops should either stock it or will order it for you specially. If you have difficulty obtaining it, write to the manufacturer (see page 158 for address). Porosan is supplied with full instructions on its use, so I won't go into that here.

For sauce making, you will require a few items of equipment in addition to the equipment used for making chutney. Firstly you will need either a mechanical sieve or an electric liquidizer. Of the two, the manual mechanical sieve is far superior, as it gives your sauce an attractive texture, whereas a liquidizer just produces an amorphous mush. You will also need a supply of bottles to put the finished sauce in, and a funnel and jug or ladle to fill them with. I find the best sort of bottles to use are glass ones with plastic coated metal screw tops; old sauce or vinegar bottles are ideal. As with the lids for chutney jars, make quite certain the plastic coating inside the metal lids is undamaged, or the vinegar will eat through the metal in no time. When the lids become too worn to be of further use, you can seal the bottles with corks and then dip the necks of the bottles in molten wax to get an airtight seal.

Once the bottles have been filled with sauce they must be sterilized. This is done by simmering the bottles in a pan of water. When choosing a sterilizing pan, make sure it's wide enough to accommodate all the bottles filled in one sauce making session. It must also be tall enough to allow the bottles to stand upright and still leave enough headroom for the lid to fit tightly. If your pan doesn't have a tightly fitting lid, a thick, folded cloth draped across the top will suffice.

You will also need some sort of trivet to prevent the bottles from coming into direct contact with the (hot) bottom of the pan, or they may crack; again, a thick, folded cloth is perfectly suitable if you don't have a proper trivet.

MAKING CHUTNEY

Preparing the ingredients

Whatever sort of chutney you are making, you will first need to chop up the ingredients, remembering to cut away carefully any decayed or damaged parts first. How you chop them up is very important. Busy people will probably use a mincer, but while you *can* do this if you like, it is far better to take a little more time and use a knife. So what's the difference? Well, the trouble with mincers is that they don't just chop, they *pulverize* as well. This ruins the distinctive shape and crispness of many ingredients, and gives the chutney an altogether flabby texture more akin to what you would buy in a supermarket. The same goes for other similar items of modern kitchen paraphernalia including the ubiquitous 'food processor'. To make really good chutney, forget all this junk and just use a sharp knife.

How finely you chop the ingredients depends on the particular ingredient in question, and how coarse or fine you like your chutney. Things like apples, that 'melt' into mush rapidly when cooked, need be no more than roughly chopped. On the other hand, tougher, more durable things like onion and (surprisingly) marrow should be chopped quite fine.

Cooking the chutney

Having chopped or minced the ingredients you should now simmer them with the spices and half the vinegar. No sweetener, whether it be malt extract, honey or brown sugar should be added yet, as it would have a toughening effect on the fruits and vegetables, especially their skins. This effect would be only very slight in the recipes given here because of the tiny amounts of these things that are called for; nonetheless, to be on the safe side don't add any sweetener until the other ingredients are either well broken down or at least quite soft. Vinegar has a similar effect, and this is why only half of it is used initially.

You should continue simmering the ingredients, stirring frequently to prevent sticking, until they are soft and

mushy; this may take up to an hour or so. If possible, cover
the pan with a lid as this will speed up the process. Once the
ingredients have softened nicely, you should add the
remaining vinegar and any sweetener called for. Remember
to remove the pan from the heat before adding the
sweetener, and stir well to make sure it has completely
dissolved.

Now return the pan to the heat and bring to a gentle boil,
stirring continuously. If your pan hasn't got a particularly
thick bottom, it is a good idea to stand it on a metal plate, as
this helps to distribute the heat and eliminate 'hot-spots', so
reducing the likelihood of the chutney sticking. Continue
boiling the chutney until there is no 'free liquid'. To test for
this, first remove the pan from the heat and give it a good
stir. Next take a teaspoonful of the chutney and put it on a
cold plate, flattening the heap of chutney slightly with the
back of the spoon. Leave the plate for five minutes to allow
the chutney to cool. Now tip the plate up steeply, if there is
any free liquid, it will run away from the main heap of
chutney. If this happens, cook the chutney for a little longer
and retest. When there is no free liquid, the chutney is ready
to pot.

Potting the chutney
Before being filled with chutney, the pots must be
thoroughly clean, dry and hot. The best way to ensure this is
to wash them in hot soapy water, rinse and drain them well
and finally, stand them in a cool oven 107°C (225°F), gas
mark ¼, for at least half an hour before they are needed.
Failure to observe these points may result in either the
chutney not keeping or the jars breaking from thermal shock
when the hot chutney is poured into them.

To pot the chutney, first give it a good stir and then
immediately pour it into the pots. I find that bailing the
chutney out with a plastic jug is a lot less trouble than using
a ladle; a jam funnel is also a great help, as it prevents
chutney getting slopped down the outside of the pots as they
are filled.

Once the pots are filled, put the lids on immediately –
needless to say, the lids should also be clean and dry. When
the last jar of chutney has been sealed, leave the jars to cool,
preferably overnight. When cold, the chutney should be
labelled and then stored away in a cool, dark and dry place
for at least three months to allow the flavours to develop.

RECIPES

Tomato chutney

5.4kg (12lb) ripe tomatoes
450g (1lb) onions
225g (½lb) seedless raisins
450g (1lb) sultanas, finely chopped
7 large cloves of garlic, finely chopped
3 tablespoons ground coriander
1 teaspoon ground cloves
1 teaspoon ground cumin
2 teaspoons ground black pepper
1 tablespoon paprika pepper
2 rounded teaspoons ground allspice
1.14 litres (2pts) malt vinegar

First peel the tomatoes by impaling each one on a fork and plunging it into a pan of boiling water for a few seconds until the skin loosens. Chop up the onions, raisins, sultanas and peeled tomatoes, and dump them into your pan, together with the chopped garlic and spices.

Pour in half the vinegar and gently heat the pan, stirring and squashing the ingredients well with your wooden spoon. When the juice starts to run, you can turn the heat up, but stir constantly to prevent sticking. As soon as the pan comes to the boil, reduce the heat and simmer gently until the ingredients are soft and mushy. Add the remainder of the vinegar, bring back to the boil, and boil gently until no free liquid remains. Pot and cover, and when cool, label the jars before storing (see page 36).

Yield: about 2.7kg (6lb).

Apple, courgette and tomato chutney

A good autumn recipe.

450g (1lb) sweet apples
450g (1lb) cooking apples
900g (2lb) courgettes
900g (2lb) ripe or green tomatoes
450g (1lb) onions
225g (8oz) sultanas, chopped
225g (8oz) sultanas, left whole
110g (4oz) seedless raisins, chopped

85g (3oz) malt extract
2 finely chopped cloves of garlic
2 teaspoons ground allspice
1 tablespoon ground fenugreek*
3 rounded teaspoons ground cumin
1 scant teaspoon ground cloves
1 rounded teaspoon ground cinnamon
1 tablespoon paprika
1 teaspoon ground black pepper
1.14 litres (2pts) malt vinegar

*If you are grinding your own spices, use the following method for the fenugreek: before grinding, roast the whole spice in a thick-bottomed pan over a gentle heat until the seeds just start to pop. Roasting really brings out the distinctive curry flavour of this spice.

Peel and core the apples, then chop them up roughly. Chop the courgettes into 0.5cm (¼″) cubes and cut the tomatoes into eighths – there is no need to peel them. Chop the onion as finely as you can, and put all the prepared fruit and vegetables into your pan together with the raisins, sultanas, chopped garlic, spices and half the vinegar. Heat the pan gently, stirring all the time, and simmer the ingredients until soft and well broken down. The softening process can be speeded up by using a potato masher to mash the ingredients from time to time. Add the malt extract and the rest of the vinegar, and cook until there is no free liquid. Pot, cover and allow to cool before labelling the jars (see page 36).
    Yield: about 3.8kg (8½lb).

Green tomato chutney

Wonderful for using up all those green tomatoes you don't know what to do with.

1.35kg (3lb) sweet apples
450g (1lb) onions
1.8kg (4lb) green (ie unripe) tomatoes
450g (1lb) cucumber
225g (8oz) sultanas
225g (8oz) seedless raisins
110g (4oz) dried stoned dates
110g (4oz) malt extract

1 tablespoon ground green cardamom
1 rounded tablespoon ground allspice
2 teaspoons ground cloves
2 tablespoons ground cinnamon
1 tablespoon ground white mustard seed
1 teaspoon cayenne pepper
1 litre (1¾pts) malt vinegar

Peel, core and chop the apples roughly. Peel the cucumber and dice into 1cm (½″) cubes. If your tomatoes are small or medium sized, halve or quarter them; larger ones should be cut into 1cm (½″) chunks. Chop the onion finely and also chop up the sultanas, raisins and dates. Place all the prepared ingredients in your pan with the spices and half the vinegar. Simmer until very soft and mushy, then add the malt extract and the remaining vinegar and cook until there is no free liquid. Pot, cover and label in the usual way (see page 36).

Yield: about 3.2kg (7lb).

Mellow plum chutney

Really delicious served with home-cured meats.

2.3kg (5lb) juicy, sweet dessert plums
450g (1lb) onions
450g (1lb) sweet apples
450g (1lb) cooking apples
450g (1lb) ripe tomatoes, peeled
450g (1lb) sultanas
110g (4oz) seedless raisins
30g (1oz) fresh root ginger
1 tablespoon ground cloves
1 teaspoon ground green cardamom
1 tablespoon ground cinnamon
1 teaspoon ground mace
2 teaspoons ground allspice
1 teaspoon grated nutmeg
850ml (1½pts) cider vinegar

Peel the ginger and cut it into slices about 0.25cm (⅛″) thick. Tie the ginger slices up in a muslin bag, leaving enough string to attach it to the handle of the pan. Cut the plums in half and remove the stones, then chop the halves roughly into 1cm (½″) chunks. Peel, core and chop the apples roughly. Chop the onion as finely as possible. If the tomatoes are fairly small, cut them in half; big ones should be cut into eighths. Place all the ingredients except half the vinegar into your pan, drop in the bag of ginger and simmer until the ingredients are soft and mushy. Add the remaining vinegar and cook until no free liquid remains. Pot and cover, and when cool, label the jars (see page 36).

Yield: about 3.5kg (8lb).

MAKING SAUCES AND KETCHUPS

The terms 'sauce' and 'ketchup' tend to be used rather interchangeably, which isn't at all surprising, as they are essentially the same thing. What *I* mean by a sauce is a thin, pourable condiment made with a variety of fruits and vegetables in such a way that no single ingredient predominates. A ketchup, on the other hand, is a sauce where a single ingredient *does* predominate.

Sauces and ketchups can be made using the same sort of recipes as you would use for chutneys. In fact, if you ever need a sauce or ketchup in a hurry, you can simply sieve or liquidize some chutney and use that. For simplicity, I shall refer only to sauce from now on, although everything I say about sauce is equally applicable to ketchups as well.

Basic procedure
First of all, wash and roughly chop the fruits and vegetables, taking care to cut out any damaged or decayed parts. Now cook them with half the vinegar until very soft – as with chutney, don't add any sweetener yet. Sieve the sauce, either with one of those clever mechanical sieves I described earlier, or by rubbing it through an ordinary sieve with a wooden spoon – alternatively, use a liquidizer. If you *do* use a liquidizer, you will almost certainly have to process the sauce in several batches, unless you have one with a really huge capacity. Pour the sieved or liquidized ingredients back into your pan, having first given the pan a quick rinse under the tap to remove any large pieces that may have clung to it. You should now add the other half of the vinegar and any sweetener called for. Boil the sauce rapidly to evaporate excess liquid, stirring continuously to prevent it from burning.

As soon as the sauce starts to thicken, you should test it from time to time to see whether all the free liquid has been

To make sauce or ketchup, first cook the ingredients gently until they are soft and mushy, then sieve, and continue cooking until there is no free liquid.

boiled off. Do this in exactly the same way you would test chutney: first remove the pan from the heat and give the sauce a good stir; then place a teaspoonful of the sauce on a cool plate and leave it for a few minutes to go cold; now tilt the plate steeply, and if liquid runs away from the main blob of sauce, it should be boiled for a little longer and then tested again; when finally there is no free liquid remaining, the sauce is ready to be bottled.

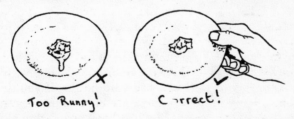

Bottling the sauce

Prepare the bottles as you would chutney pots, to ensure they are scrupulously clean, dry and hot. When you have done this, pour the sauce into them using a jug and funnel, then screw the tops down firmly.

Most sauces will keep well without further treatment, but as a precaution it is as well to sterilize all your sauces as follows. First stand the bottles in your sterilizing pan, remembering to use a trivet or folded cloth to prevent them from coming into direct contact with the bottom. Now loosen the tops about a quarter turn and fill the pan with *hot* water (about 77°C (170°F) if you've got a thermometer – don't worry if you haven't). The hot water should come up to the same level as the sauce inside the bottles. Put the lid on the pan tightly, bring the water to simmering point, then continue simmering the bottles for half an hour. At the end of this time, remove the bottles from the pan and screw the tops down hard. Leave over night to cool, then label the bottles and store in a cool, dark place for a couple of months before use.

RECIPES

Tomato ketchup

Once you've tasted this you'll wonder how you ever put up with the rubbish in the shops! A word of caution, however: unless you either grow your own tomatoes or can get them fairly cheaply, this recipe can work out a little pricey.

4.5kg (10lb) very ripe tomatoes
450g (1lb) shallots or onions
3 tablespoons honey
2 cloves of garlic, finely chopped
2 rounded tablespoons ground coriander
large sprig of tarragon, finely chopped or 2 tablespoons of
 tarragon vinegar
570ml (1pt) cider or white wine vinegar

Chop the shallots or onions as finely as possible. Chop the tomatoes roughly. Place the prepared onion, tomatoes, tarragon or tarragon vinegar and garlic in your pan, together with the coriander and half the vinegar. Heat the pan gently, stirring all the time. Once the juice begins to run, the heat can be turned up, but continue to stir. Cook gently until the ingredients are very soft and mushy, then sieve and return to the pan. Add the honey and the balance of the vinegar, and stir well to dissolve the honey. Boil gently, stirring continuously until no free liquid remains, then bottle, sterilize and leave to cool. When the bottles are cold, label them and store in a cool, dark place until required (see page 36).

  Yield: about 1.4 litres (2½pts).

Sharp plum sauce

This sauce is a very good accompaniment to cold meats.

2.3kg (5lb) sweet plums
285g (10oz) onions
110g (4oz) dried currants
110g (4oz) sultanas
110g (4oz) finely chopped dried apricot
2 tablespoons honey
1 tablespoon ground coriander
1 tablespoon ground mace
1 teaspoon ground cloves
½ teaspoon ground ginger
570ml (1pt) cider or white wine vinegar

Wash and stone the plums, then cut them up roughly and place in the pan. Chop the onion finely and add to the pan, together with the currants, sultanas, chopped apricot and spices. Pour on half the vinegar and heat the pan gently, stirring well to prevent sticking. When the ingredients come to the boil, reduce the heat and simmer until everything has softened well; this should take between thirty minutes and an hour. Now sieve the ingredients and return to the pan. Add the honey and the remainder of the vinegar, and boil gently, stirring all the time, until no free liquid remains. Bottle, sterilize and label the bottles when cool (see page 36).
Yield: about 1.7 litres (3pts).

Fruit sauce

1.35kg (3lb) sweet plums
1.8kg (4lb) red tomatoes
900g (2lb) cooking apples
900g (2lb) sweet apples
900g (2lb) shallots or onions
450g (1lb) stoned dates
450g (1lb) seedless raisins
900g (2lb) sultanas
225g (8oz) dried apricots
30g (1oz) garlic, finely chopped
2 tablespoons ground allspice
1 teaspoon ground cloves
3 rounded teaspoon ground ginger
1 teaspoon ground green cardamom

½ teaspoon ground cumin
½ teaspoon ground mace
570ml (1pt) cider vinegar
570ml (1pt) malt vinegar

Halve the plums and remove the stones, then chop the halved plums roughly. Peel and chop the shallots or onions finely; also peel and core the apples and cut into 1cm (½″) chunks. Cut the tomatoes into quarters and chop the dates and apricots finely. Place the prepared ingredients in your pan, with the raisins, sultanas, garlic and spices. Add the malt vinegar and bring to simmering point over a gentle heat, stirring continuously. When everything is soft and mushy, sieve and return to the pan. Pour in the cider vinegar and boil until there is no free liquid, then bottle, sterilize and label in the usual way (see page 36).

   Yield: about 4.8 litres (8½pts).

Gooseberry ketchup

1.8kg (4lb) ripe gooseberries
560g (1¼lb) sultanas
450g (1lb) onions
1 tablespoon honey
3 teaspoons ground cinnamon
2 teaspoons ground mace
2 teaspoons grated nutmeg
1 teaspoon ground cloves
2 teaspoons ground white mustard seed
1 teaspoon ground ginger
850ml (1½pts) cider vinegar

Top and tail the gooseberries and place in the pan. Chop the onions and add to the pan with the sultanas and spice. Pour on half the vinegar and bring the ingredients to simmering point over a gentle heat. Simmer gently, stirring frequently, and when soft enough to do so, mash the gooseberries occasionally with a potato masher. Continue simmering until the ingredients are really soft and mushy. Sieve, and then return to the pan, adding the remaining vinegar and the honey. Stir well to dissolve the honey, then return to the heat and boil gently until no free liquid remains, stirring continuously. Bottle, sterilize and label when cool (see page 36).

   Yield: about 2.3 litres (4pts).

3.
SAUSAGES
AND BURGERS

BANGERS AND TRASH

Have you ever wondered what goes into a typical
supermarket sausage or burger? If you have a look at the
label, you will probably feel reassured to see that there
appears to be a high percentage of meat. But what exactly
does the term 'meat' mean? To you and I, meat is the stuff
we see in chunks on the local butcher's slab, but if you think
that's all there is to it, then you're in for a big shock! The
food regulations (Meat Products and Spreadable Fish
Products Regulations 1984, SI No 1566 HMSO) allow the
meat industry to use all sorts of ingredients – many of which
would once have been sent to the knacker's yard as rubbish
– and get away with calling them meat. For instance, fat,
skin, gristle and sinew are all meat as far as the regulations
and the meat industry are concerned, and the diaphragm,
head meat, heart, kidney, liver, pancreas, tail meat, thymus
and tongue – and in poultry the gizzard, heart, liver and
neck – are all meat as well! Worse still, in cooked meat
products made from an animal other than a bird, the brains,
feet, intestines, lungs, oesophagus, rectum, spinal chord,
spleen, stomach, testicles and udder can all be used as
legitimate ingredients – although not even the food industry
can get away with calling these things meat.

Fair enough, some of these things are wholesome – like
the kidneys and liver – but even so, only the meat industry
would ever think of them as meat, and to describe them as
such is a gross and despicable deception of the public. And as
far as the rubbish is concerned, the only clause controlling
its completely unrestrained use is the requirement that
these repugnant scraps may only be present '. . . in amounts

naturally associated with the flesh used . . .', yet another conveniently vague piece of gobbledegook from the Ministry of Agriculture. What this definition presumably means is that you could remove from an animal the very few things not construed to be meat, mince up what's left and quite legally sell it as meat in the form of sausages, burgers and other meat products.

Needless to say, the food manufacturers make full use of this rather catholic definition when concocting their sausage and burger recipes, and produce some of the most tasteless and repugnant abominations ever to be sold as food. To give an example, the typical supermarket beef sausage need by law contain only 50 per cent 'meat', and of this, only half has to be lean, or in other words what you or I would consider meat. The rest of the 'meat' can be either just fat, or else a mixture of fat and the other nasties mentioned above, as long as they are used in amounts 'naturally associated with the flesh concerned'. The remaining 50 per cent of the sausage is invariably a mixture of cereal products like rusk, added to make the 'meat' go further, water (that's even cheaper than cereal extenders), more fat and a sprinkling of additives including colour and flavour enhancer to hide some of the blandness, and of course polyphosphates to enable it to hold plenty of water. Last but not least, antioxidants and preservatives are added to try to prevent the whole unsavoury horror from going bad.

Of course, what I have just outlined is a rather optimistic view of the supermarket sausage; after all, I have described what the law says these sausages should be, and not everybody obeys the law, do they? To make matters worse, it is very difficult for those whose job it is to enforce the law to determine exactly what a sausage or burger contains, and so there is indeed great scope for the law to be broken. For example, ground-up bone cannot legally be added to meat products unless it is declared on the label, but it can easily be added and go undetected, especially now the industry has the technology to 'recover' previously wasted pieces of meat attached to bone, usually by either grinding the whole lot to pulp or else by scraping it off. The use of this Mechanically Recovered Meat (or MRM as it is known in the industry) is as yet unregulated in this country, and can pass as ordinary lean meat on the list of ingredients.

The situation is exactly the same for burgers, except that all but 'economy' burgers have to contain at least 80 per cent meat, 65 per cent of which has to be lean; economy burgers only have to have a measly 60 per cent meat content, and only 65 per cent of that has to be lean. This means that many burgers only contain a pitiful 39 per cent of what you or I would recognize as meat.

HOMEMADE SAUSAGES AND BURGERS

In sharp contrast to the repugnance of the commercial products, homemade sausages and burgers can contain as much meat as you like, and I mean *meat*, not knacker's scraps. More often than not *you* will want to make the meat go a bit further as a matter of economy – but with wholesome things like oats and wholemeal breadcrumbs, not fat, water and polyphosphates. You can give your sausages and burgers extra flavour with herbs, spices or even wine, and blend in other ingredients like chopped peppers and tomatoes to make them uniquely your own. In fact, when I make sausages and burgers I rarely follow a recipe to the letter and frequently add various little extras as the mood takes me.

EQUIPMENT FOR SAUSAGE AND BURGER MAKING

The only special item of equipment that is pretty much essential is a mincer. If you don't already have one, then you can always manage without and buy your meat ready-minced instead. But the trouble with buying your meat ready-minced is that you can't always tell how much fat the butcher has used, and from a health point of view the less that's in it the better. Price is usually a good guide, though; the more the mince costs the less fatty it is likely to be. If you have a choice, ask for the best quality mince, or better still, ask your butcher to mince the meat of your choice specially. Most butchers will do this for you if your order is large enough.

The other snag with having to buy your meat ready-minced is that it limits your choice of meat; after all, how many butchers would cheerfully bone and mince poultry or game for you? The best thing to do, then, is buy your own mincer and do it yourself.

Choosing a mincer
The most common sort of mincer uses two metal plates to cut

the meat, one of which is fixed while the other rotates. Although mincers of this kind are fine for cooked meats they don't cope with raw meat that well, especially when the edges of the holes in the plates become blunt with use. The other sort uses a rotating knife to do the cutting, and is far superior; if you are going to buy a mincer, this is the kind to go for.

Having decided to buy the rotating knife type of mincer, you now have to choose between hand-cranked and electric models. Unless you are going to mince really large amounts of meat regularly, a hand-cranked mincer is perhaps your best bet. The drawback with the hand-operated mincer is that when you are making sausages you will need two people to do it: one of you will have to turn the handle and manipulate the sausage skins while the other spoons the sausage mixture into the mincer. If you don't have another person on hand, you had better opt for a small electric mincer. Whether you buy an electric or a hand mincer, though, make sure there is a sausage-filling nozzle available for it or you won't be able to use it to fill the skins.

If you intend to make burgers, you should consider investing in a burger press. While this isn't in any way essential, it will allow you to make nice, neat burgers which tend to hold together better when you cook them and take up less room in the deep freeze if you decide to make a large batch and freeze some. Using a press also speeds up the process of burger making.

MAKING BURGERS

You can use any sort of meat you like to make burgers, but the most commonly used are beef and pork, either on their own or in combination. To make your chosen meat go a bit further you can add things like wholemeal breadcrumbs or rolled oats. You can even add a little of your favourite ketchup, chutney or relish; tomato ketchup is very good for beef burgers. To bring out the flavour of the meat properly you should always use plenty of herbs and spices in your recipes; thyme, sage, marjoram, rosemary, parsley and garlic are among my favourite herbs, and mace, allspice, coriander, fenugreek, cardamom, cumin, capers and cloves are all good burger spices. If at all possible, use only fresh herbs and grind the spices freshly. You can also add finely chopped vegetables of your choice; sweet peppers are very suitable and I always use a generous amount of chopped onion in my burgers.

There is one point, however, that you should always bear in mind when making burgers: the more non-meat ingredients you include, and the more coarsely it is all chopped and minced, the greater the tendency for the burgers to fall apart while being cooked. So to help to bind them together, it is usually a good idea to mix in some beaten egg: use about one egg for each 450–675g (1–1½lb) of burger mixture. Putting the mixture through the fine plate of your mincer is often a good idea if your burgers look a little fragile. Using a proper press also helps to produce nice, firm burgers.

As a general rule, keep the cereal content of the burgers to no more than about 15 per cent of the weight of the meat. As for any vegetables used (including onion), add no more than a quarter of the weight of the meat. If you mince your own meat, you should remember to mince a little fat with any very lean meat; ask your butcher for some or use a little grated or shredded suet. Burgers made from completely lean meat will be very dry and unappetizing, and this is especially the case with game and most poultry meats. If you do need to add some fat, then depending on how lean the meat is, you should use up to about 85g (3oz) for every 450g (1lb) of meat.

Choice of meat

You can use any type of meat or mixture of meats you fancy, although beef and pork will be the most usual choice. To make really special burgers, use game or poultry meats, either on their own or combined with beef or pork. Remember that game and most poultry meats tend to be very dry, and so will need to have fat added.

You can use any cut of meat you like, but as a general rule, the cheaper, fattier cuts make the tastiest and most juicy burgers; shin beef and belly pork are good cuts to choose. If you are using very lean game or poultry meats, then mixing them with an equal quantity of belly pork is a very good way of ensuring your burgers are really succulent.

Basic recipe

This recipe is for *beef* burgers, but you could equally well use other meats.

900g (2lb) shin beef or minced beef, not too lean
110g (4oz) oatmeal or wholemeal breadcrumbs
2 eggs, beaten
170g (6oz) minced or finely chopped onion
4 cloves of finely chopped garlic
4 tablespoons fresh or dried parsley, chopped
2 teaspoons ground mace
2 tablespoons of paprika
1 teaspoon of ground cloves
2 teaspoons of ground coriander
4 teaspoons of capers (optional)

Assuming you are mincing your own meat, trim off any
gristle and sinew and put the beef thorough the fine plate of
your mincer. Cut the capers into quarters, then chop the
garlic as fine as possible and crush it with the side of your
knife. Place everything in a bowl and mix throughly. If you
have a mincer, you can, if you wish, pass the whole mixture
through the fine plate to give the burgers a finer texture,
but this isn't essential. The mixture should be sticky enough
to hold together if you squeeze it, but if it's too dry, add a
little milk, wine or even sauce or ketchup, taking care not to
overdo it. If the mixture is too wet and sticky, add some
breadcrumbs to dry it off.

Once the mixture has the correct consistency, it should be
formed into burger shapes using either your hands or a
burger press. Ideally, you should leave the burgers overnight
in a cool place for the flavour to develop before cooking
them. But if you're in a hurry to try one – and you no doubt
will be! – they can be cooked and eaten right away.

MAKING SAUSAGES

Sausages are made using the same sorts of recipe you would
use for burgers, but instead of being formed into burger
shapes the mixture is forced into sausage skins or 'cases'.
Traditionally, these cases were the intestines of various
animals, notably the pig, although synthetic cellulose ones
are often found round supermarket sausages. Traditional
cases can sometimes be a little difficult to find, but a good
butcher – especially one that makes his own sausages – may
be able to get them for you. (Failing that, see Further
Information on page 158 for the name and address of a
supplier.)

Wherever you get your cases from, they will come packed either in brine or dry salt. You should remember that they are, by their very nature, decidedly inclined to go 'off', and so require careful handling. If your cases are in (more or less) dry salt when you get them, then sprinkle 1cm (½″) of salt in a suitably sized clean glass or pottery jar and tip the cases into it. Now bury them with another 1cm of salt, pressing them down well. If they're in brine, drain this off first before packing them in dry salt. Keep the jar covered with a close fitting lid to keep flies and dampness out, and store in a cool, dark place – but not the fridge. Stored in this way, the cases will sometimes keep for as long as two years, although to be on the safe side try not to buy more than you think you will use up within six months or so. If you do keep them too long, it's easy to tell if they've gone off, since when this happens they turn a distinctly pink colour and must then be thrown away.

Banger recipes

The most commonly used meat for sausages is pork. Pork lends itself well to sausage making because it is a rather fatty and relatively bland meat which readily takes on the flavours and aromas of other more flavoursome ingredients such as herbs and spices. Also, on account of their high fat content, sausages made with pork are always succulent and juicy. Sausages made from a mixture of pork and game meats are delicious beyond description.

As far as choosing cuts of meat is concerned, generally use the same cheap and fatty cuts as you would use for burgers, and if the meat is very lean, add up to 85g (3oz) of fat per 450g (1lb) of meat, depending on leanness; as with burgers, either mince some fat from the butcher or use shredded suet.

Marinades

A very effective way of tenderizing and adding extra flavour to cheap cuts of meat is to marinade the meat overnight, or even for as long as a couple of days, before making the sausages. Although you can easily devise your own marinade recipe, a good general-purpose one can be made by combining in a small bowl 150ml (¼pt) of dry or sweet wine, 3 tablespoons of olive oil, 1 teaspoon of Worcestershire Sauce or Shoyu (high quality soya sauce available from wholefood shops and delicatessens) and 1 tablespoon of lemon juice. Add to this a finely chopped sprig of thyme, sage, rosemary

or marjoram, and one crushed clove of garlic. Now add ½
teaspoon of ground mace and ½ teaspoon of ground black
peppercorns. Mix everything together well and the marinade
is ready to use. The quantities given will be sufficient to
marinade up to 675g (1½lb) of meat.

Pork and beef sausage

Although this recipe uses a mixture of pork and beef, you
could equally well use just pork or beef on its own, or indeed
any other sort of meat or mixture of meats of your choice. If
at all possible, grind the spices freshly in either a spice mill
or a coffee grinder.

450g (1lb) shin beef
450g (1lb) belly pork
110g (4oz) coarse oatmeal, rolled oats or wholemeal
  breadcrumbs
110g (4oz) finely chopped onion
3 cloves garlic
4 tablespoons tomato ketchup
4 teaspoons finely chopped fresh or dried thyme
2 teaspoons ground mace
4 teaspoons ground allspice
3 teaspoons ground black pepper
1 teaspoon ground ginger
3 teaspoons grated nutmeg
2 teaspoons ground cinnamon
1½ teaspoons ground cloves
marinade (optional) – see page 51

Slice the meat into 2½cm wide strips, excluding any skin,
gristle or bone. The meat can now be marinaded for 24 hours
if desired using the recipe given on page 51, but this is not
essential.

After marinading, mince the meat, using the fine plate of
your mincer. Now either mince or chop the onion finely and
put the minced meat, minced or chopped onion, the oatmeal
or breadcrumbs and the tomato ketchup into a large mixing
bowl. Chop the garlic fine and add it to the bowl along with
the chopped thyme and all the spices. Mix everything
together very thoroughly, and then put the whole lot
through the mincer again using the fine plate. If after
mincing the mixture is a little dry, moisten it with some
left-over marinade or some milk or wine, but take care not

to add too much; the mixture should be sticky but not wet.

You are now ready to fill the cases with the mixture, but first you must prepare the cases. Do this by taking out of your jar the length of case you think you'll need (every 450g (1lb) sausage mixture needs approximately 90cm (3 feet) casing), and washing the salt off under the cold tap. Now, with the tap still running, take a length of casing and thread one end of it onto the tap so as to run water through it. Close the other end with your fingers, and when the case has a little water in it, take it off the tap and pinch this end closed as well. Now run the trapped water to and fro inside the case by raising and lowering your hands so that you can find any holes there may be in it. In the unlikely event that there are a great many, you will have to discard the whole piece of case. If there are just one or two, cut the case into smaller pieces at the points where the leaks are. You should repeat this process with the other lengths and then soak the prepared cases in cold water until required.

While the cases are soaking, fit the sausage nozzle to the mincer. With some mincers you will have to remove the rotary blade and the plate in order to do this; with others you must leave them in place. Once you've fitted the sausage nozzle, thread a length of prepared case onto it and then switch on the mincer, or start turning the handle if it's a hand-operated one, and feed the sausage mixture into it. As soon as you see the mixture just beginning to emerge from the end of the nozzle, switch off, or stop turning the handle, and tie a knot in the end of the case.

You can now begin to fill the case. Do this by slowly feeding the mixture into the mincer and at the same time supporting the case as it begins to fill. By regulating how fast the case runs off the nozzle you can control the thickness of your sausage, but be careful not to overfill it as it may burst when you divide it into links. Fill the cases slowly at first until you start to get the hang of it, and don't worry if your sausage isn't of a nice even thickness – that will come with practice.

When you come to the end of the first length of case, remove it from the nozzle and tie a knot in the open end. Put the filled case on one side, fit another length onto the nozzle and continue as before. When you get to the end of the sausage mixture, force what still remains in the nozzle into the case using the handle of a wooden spoon, being careful not to get air trapped in the sausage.

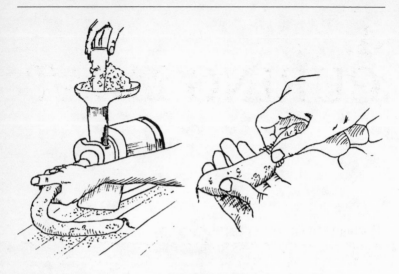

First fill the sausage skins, then pinch and twist them into links every four inches or so.

Once the cases have been filled, divide the lengths of sausage into links by carefully pinching the sausage and then twisting at about four inch intervals. Put the finished sausage into a clean bowl and leave overnight in a cool place for the flavours to mature and integrate properly – if you can wait that long! If you can't, you can cook them right away, although you won't be tasting them at their best.

FREEZING BURGERS AND SAUSAGES

If you have a deep freeze, it makes sense to make your burgers and sausages in large batches and freeze what you don't need immediately for future use. Both burgers and sausages will keep well for up to two months, after which their flavour starts to deteriorate. Before freezing them, remember to let them stand overnight to mature, then divide them into usable amounts and freeze as quickly as possible.

A TIP WITH MINCERS

To get the very last of your burger or sausage mixture out of your mincer, feed in a little wholemeal bread at the end to expel any mixture still inside.

4.
CURING MEAT

Curing is the process of preserving meat with salt: quite simply, if you make a piece of meat salty enough it will keep indefinitely – provided it is subsequently kept dry and free of pests like flies and rodents.

Given that nowadays we have deep-freezes and refrigerators to do the job of preserving our meat, you might think that curing is something of an anachronism. And were it not for the fact that curing doesn't merely preserve meat but enhances its flavour as well, then it would no doubt have given way totally to the icy incursions of the deep-freeze. Instead, curing meat is still very big business today; in Britain in 1986 alone, the retail value of bacon and ham was in excess of £1,200,000,000!

Curing works because the moulds and bacteria that would otherwise attack the meat cannot survive in very salty conditions. However, although salt is a first-rate natural preservative it can only do its job effectively if it gets into the meat quickly, and in the correct amounts; knowing how best to ensure this is what curing is all about.

METHODS OF CURING

Dry and Wet Curing

In its simplest form, curing merely entails rubbing your chosen piece of meat with salt; this is called 'dry' curing. Alternatively, you can dissolve the salt in water and steep the meat in the resulting brine; this is 'wet' curing. It is possible to cure using salt alone, but more usually the cure is a mixture of things. Curing mixtures still consist mainly of salt since this is the essential preservative, but they also contain a proportion of sugar as well. If used in large enough amounts, sugar would act as a sweetener, but in smaller amounts its main purpose is to tenderize the meat; bacteria in the meat convert sugars into organic acids, and these acids break the meat down slightly, giving it a softer texture. This is important, because salt has completely the opposite effect, tending to harden the meat considerably; a little sugar in the cure helps to offset this.

As far as traditional curing is concerned, there are two other ingredients commonly included in the curing mixture: spice and, possibly, herbs, and saltpetre (sodium or potassium nitrate). The spices and herbs are there simply to enhance the flavour of the meat; the saltpetre is altogether more questionable, but more about that later.

Factory curing
The vast majority of cured meat sold in Britain – mostly ham and bacon – is not cured in the traditional way, but made on large-scale production lines. In these large factories, gone are considerations of flavour and quality; profitability and speed of throughput reign supreme. Once upon a time it was an offence to dilute food with water – indeed for some commodities like beer this is still the case. But no longer is this so with cured meats. Though the industry obviously wouldn't admit that there is anything wrong with what it does, the meat industry none the less systematically defrauds the consumer by deliberately adding water to its meat. In its quest to cram water into its products, the industry even enlists the help of special chemicals called polyphosphates (notably E450 (a), (b) and (c)), which have the property of making meat hold more water than it otherwise could, thereby artificially increasing its weight and hence the profit when it is sold to the unsuspecting public. As well as using chemicals, the meat industry has learned another little trick: if the meat is bashed around a bit – or, in the jargon the meat trade prefers to use, 'massaged' or 'tumbled' – this too increases its water-holding capacity by virtue of the fact that this sort of assault treatment tends to render the meat a spongy, amorphous mush.

Not surprisingly, the manufacturers exploit this new profit-making potential to the full by adding as much water to the meat as they can get away with. Anyone who doubts that this flagrant – though perfectly legal – dishonesty goes on, should look at any meat industry journal or textbook; a book on commercial bacon production that I read recently had a section entitled *Increasing your Yields by Using Additives*, and an advertisement in a meat trades journal proclaimed 'Why sell meat when you can sell water?'! In 1979, *Which?* magazine found that some brands of canned ham contained as much as 42 per cent water! But that's nothing, the meat industry has the technology to put in nearly twice that amount!

NITRATES AND NITROSAMINES

Nitrates

The early exponents of the art of curing noticed that their meat sometimes took on a distinctly rosy hue that remained even when the meat had been cooked. Though they didn't realize it at the time, this pigmentation was due to the presence of nitrate impurities in the salt, or perhaps the water, they used to cure the meat. As soon as this was known, the cosmetic use of nitrates very soon became standard, the nitrate traditionally taking the form of saltpetre.

Eventually it became apparent that the nitrate was only indirectly responsible for giving the meat its pink colour; it was in fact nitrites produced by bacteria in the meat acting on the nitrate which were responsible. The nitrite gives the meat its pink colour by preventing oxygen from combining with two pigments in the meat called *myoglobin* and *haemoglobin*; if oxidized, these would turn brown. Unfortunately, when food containing nitrites are eaten, the nitrites behave in exactly the same way in our bodies, preventing the haemoglobin in our blood from doing its vital job of carrying oxygen to our tissues and organs. As you would expect, if you were to ingest enough nitrite you would die of nitrite asphyxiation – although admittedly you would have to eat a terrific amount of cured meat before this became a possibility. More typical symptoms from eating moderate amounts of these foods would be headaches, dizziness and nausea. Babies and small children are particularly at risk, and should never under any circumstances be given foods containing these additives. Despite this, I have never yet seen cured meats labelled with warnings of this danger.

Nitrosamines

Perhaps even more worryingly, nitrites have the ability to combine with *amines* (basic proteins) present either in the meat itself or in the food in our stomachs, to form particularly toxic substances called *nitrosamines*. Nitrosamines have long been known to be highly potent carcinogens (cancer causers), and have been found to be present in cured meats and other foods which contain added nitrates or nitrites. Even as far back as 1968, the British medical journal *the Lancet* expressed grave concern about nitrosamines in food. Added to the nitrosamine danger, there is evidence that nitrites might in themselves be carcinogenic, irrespective of their ability to form nitrosamines.

Cured meat is not the only source of nitrates and nitrites in our diet; in fact, something like three-quarters of our nitrate intake is from vegetables – especially those grown with large amounts of nitrate fertilizers. The food industry has argued that this is precisely why we shouldn't worry about the nitrate and nitrite additives they put into our food. But really the converse is true: if we do get such large doses of these potentially highly toxic nitrates from vegetables – something we can't do much about – then we must severely reduce our intake from other sources, and this we *can* do something about.

It has never been more important to reduce our intake of nitrates than it is today, especially in view of the rapidly escalating concentrations of nitrates in our drinking water from the leaching and run-off of agricultural fertilizers. The food companies refuse to admit that the main reason for using nitrates and nitrites in cured meats is purely cosmetic: perhaps they feel threatened that people would be less inclined to buy bacon and ham that is brown or tan in colour rather than the bright pink they have become accustomed to. Instead, they point to the fact that nitrites prevent the growth of certain bacteria in the meat. But whether the food technologists like it or not, people have, and still do, cure meats without the use of these dangerous additives, and provided your meat is properly cooked there is no danger whatever in omitting nitrates and nitrites. If you think about it, it's exactly the same with poultry: if it is not properly cooked then you may well give yourself salmonella food poisoning, but so long as it *is* cooked properly, there isn't the remotest chance of this happening.

CURING AT HOME

By doing your own curing, not only can you avoid the dangerous nitrates and nitrites, you can also save a lot of money as well. Supermarket ham costs you around twice what it would cost to make your own, yet it is pumped full of water, making it appear cheaper per pound than it really is.

In days of yore, when the household hog was a common sight, it was usual to slaughter the animal towards the end of the year, when the weather was getting decidedly chilly at the onset of winter. One of the reasons for this was that a lot of the meat would be cured into bacon and ham, and as it takes a considerable time for the salt to permeate the meat sufficiently to prevent putrefaction, the meat must be kept cold, to minimize any danger of it going bad before the salt has done its work. And so, since refrigerators hadn't yet been invented, curing had to be left until the cold weather arrived. If you have a refrigerator there is no need to wait for a cold snap; you can cure your bacon and ham – or for that matter any other sort of meat – whenever you fancy.

Although keeping the meat cool *is* very important, I have on a couple of occasions successfully cured bacon in the height of summer without a fridge – though I would definitely advise against trying this yourself. With larger pieces of meat, which take longer for the salt to penetrate than with relatively thin bacon, you must *never* attempt to cure unless you can keep the temperature down reliably. The ideal temperature for curing is between 2 and 4°C (36–39°F). At much lower than 2°C the meat will not take the cure properly, and under no circumstances should you let the meat freeze, as frozen meat won't take the cure at all.

Equipment for curing

The first thing you will need is a cold place to keep the meat in. This means either waiting until winter or using a refrigerator. If you choose the latter, an ordinary domestic fridge is fine for the job, provided the thermostat can be set low enough (do make sure of this, as many so-called 'larder' fridges cannot be set to a sufficiently low temperature). Check with a thermometer that the temperature is between 2 and 4°C.

Just about the only other piece of equipment you will need is some sort of container to stand the meat in. If you are going to use the wet method (see below), make certain that the container is big enough to allow the meat to be covered by 5cm (2″) or so of the curing solution without the container being so full that the solution slops out all over the place when you move it around. If you are using the dry method, the container can be quite shallow, and need only be wide enough to hold the meat. In either case, the most likely choice of container will be a food-grade plastic bucket. The best place to get one of these is a shop that sells home brewing equipment; you can then be certain the plastic is safe for food use. Obviously, you should never use a metal container as the salt will attack it.

If you intend to cure by the wet method, there are a couple of other items you will need – but more about those later.

Wet or dry curing?

Dry curing is faster than the wet process and so leaves less time for unwelcome bacteria to spoil the meat. For this reason, always use the dry method if you cannot keep the temperature down to the recommended 2–4°C (36–39°F). If you have never cured before, I would suggest you have a go at dry curing first; it is slightly simpler than the wet method, and provided you pay attention to detail there is virtually nothing to go wrong.

Choice of meat

Any type or cut of meat can be cured by either the wet or dry method, but bear in mind that it isn't really worth the trouble to cure a piece of meat weighing less that about 1.8kg (4lb), and that cheaper cuts usually cure better than very lean, expensive cuts. Until you have gained a little confidence, it is a good idea to restrict yourself to smallish pieces of meat, leaving the curing of large hams until you've had more practice. Pig has always been the favourite meat for curing, and is a good choice to start with. A good cut of pork to try is loin; this will make wonderful bacon. If you are feeling more adventurous and fancy trying something a little more unusual, then a whole leg of lamb makes a delicious 'ham' with a distinctive gamey flavour. To make real ham though, you will have to use a whole leg of pork. Whatever sort of meat you buy, it is always a good idea to tell the butcher you intend to cure it; a knowledgeable butcher will often cut the meat differently, according to how you are going to use it.

INGREDIENTS FOR CURING

Salt

The most important ingredient in curing is salt. If at all possible, use good quality rock salt for all your curing, whether it be by the dry or wet method. The advantage of using rock salt is that it is mined from the deposits of seas that have long since dried up, and not made by evaporating our present-day highly polluted ones. If you simply can't get rock salt, or it is too expensive, then use fine sea salt. Ordinary table and cooking salts are to be avoided as they invariably contain undesirable additives.

Sugar

Although not strictly essential, sugar has a tenderizing effect on the meat, so it is a good idea to use a little, although it can be left out if you prefer. The best sort to use is one of the *genuine* Barbados or Muscavado sugars, which come in various shades of brown, the darker ones having more flavour. To check that it is the genuine article, look to see if there is a country of origin on the bag. If there isn't, then it's just white sugar dyed with molasses and it will have little more flavour than (cheaper) white sugar.

Saltpetre

I think I've said enough about nitrates and nitrites already to persuade you to avoid this dangerous and unnecessary additive. There can be a price to pay for not using saltpetre, but happily it need only be a cosmetic one. It just means that instead of being bright pink, your cured meat will look somewhat grey or tan in colour. This is something you very quickly get used to, and in no way harms the flavour; after all, some of the world-famous British hams, such as Bradenham, are virtually coal-black because of the molasses used to cure them, so why worry? Use some really dark sugar – even treacle or molasses – in the cure, and make a virtue of the dark colour!

If you do want a lighter colour, a little trick I learned a couple of years ago is to include some ascorbic acid (vitamin C) in the cure; this definitely seems to minimize the greying effect. If you want light-coloured or more delicately flavoured meats, don't use dark sugars; use the white kind, or a light-coloured honey.

Spices and herbs

About the only other thing you might want to include in your curing mixture are herbs and spices, to add a little extra flavour. Good spices to use are mace, nutmeg, cloves, fenugreek, cardamom, coriander, juniper berries (very good for bacon and ham), peppercorns, cinnamon and ginger. Whatever spices you choose, make sure you buy them whole and *not* ground.

If you want to use herbs as well as or instead of the spice, make sure you choose only very strongly flavoured or aromatic ones such as rosemary, sage, dill, thyme, tarragon and garlic. If at all possible, use only fresh herbs as they need to be as pungent as possible to flavour the meat well.

DRY CURING

Dry curing is the fastest and simplest way to cure meat; as I said above, if curing is new to you, then this is the method to try first. Choose a small piece of meat to start with, like some loin or belly pork, or a small leg of lamb.

Making up the cure

Clearly, the amount of salt you use for a given weight of meat is of critical importance. Too little salt, and the meat will not cure sufficiently and will go bad. Too much, and the meat will not only taste very salty, but it will be hard and dry as well. The rule for dry curing, irrespective of the type or cut of meat you are using, is 370g (13oz) of salt for each 4.5kg (10lb) of meat. Similarly, for each 4.5kg of meat you should use 85–110g (3–4oz) of sugar or honey of your choice.

If you want a light-coloured meat, remember to use white sugar or a light honey, and use some ascorbic acid as well; for ever 4.5kg of meat you should use 4g (⅛oz) of ascorbic acid. Buy the ascorbic acid in crystalline form from a chemist, *not* as vitamin C tablets. If you can't weigh these small amounts out yourself, remember as a rough guide that one level teaspoonful is about 5g (⅙oz). There's no need to be over-fussy in measuring the ascorbic acid; you can't do any harm by using slightly too much or too little.

Finally, there are the spices and herbs to consider. What you use is up to you, but nutmeg, mace, cardamom, cloves and juniper berries are amongst my favourites. You should allow 55–110g (2–4oz) of spices of your choice for each 4.5kg (10lb) of meat, and go easy on the juniper berries if you use them, as these can easily spoil the meat with their overpowering gin flavour; use no more than half an ounce for 4.5kg of meat.

If you want to use herbs, then two small handfuls of the fresh sort should be enough for a 4.5kg piece of meat – use even more if you wish. If you can't get fresh herbs, use about two tablespoons of dried herbs per 450g (1lb) of meat.

Dry curing in practice

Having weighed out the correct amounts of salt, sugar and spices, put the salt and sugar into a bowl. Crush (*not* grind) the spices slightly by wrapping them in a clean cloth, and pound them with a rolling pin. Now empty the crushed spices into the bowl. If you are using herbs, chop them finely and add these to the bowl also. Now mix everything together well and divide the mixture into two roughly equal parts, leaving one half in the bowl and putting the other into a jar with an airtight lid for use later.

Next, stand the meat in the bucket (or whatever you are going to cure it in), first making sure that the bucket has been thoroughly cleaned with very hot soapy water, and rinsed well to remove all traces of soap which would otherwise taint the meat. Holding the meat with one hand, rub the half of the cure left in the bowl into the meat with your other hand. Using a gentle massaging action, rub the cure carefully into all parts of the meat including any skin there may be. You should rub more into the thicker parts and less into the thinner parts. Take care to force some cure into any holes or cavities, as this is where putrefaction can set in and ruin the whole piece of meat. Make sure that any cavities left by the removal of bones receive an especially generous amount. If the meat still has a bone in it – as for instance a leg of lamb will have – pack a little cure into any places where the meat is coming away from the bone.

Now place the meat skin-side down in your bucket, and cover with a fly-proof cover; a piece of muslin tied over the top is better than an air-tight lid, since without some ventilation the meat tends to become mouldy. The meat should then be placed in your fridge (or another cool place), and kept at a temperature between 2–4°C (36–39°F) or at least very close to this.

The following day, you should rub the meat all over with any cure and juices that have come off it. On the next (that is, the third) day, for joints that initially weighed less than about 3.6kg (8lb), rub in the whole jar of cure you set aside earlier. For joints heavier than this, rub only half of the cure into the meat. Although there may be only a small amount of cure, try to get some of it on each part of the meat, paying most attention to the thicker parts.

Continue rubbing the meat each day as before. On the tenth day, if all the cure hasn't already been used, rub in the remaining portion. Thereafter, keep rubbing the meat each day until the meat is fully cured.

Curing times

How long this will take depends on how thick and fatty the meat is; the thicker or fattier it is, the longer it will take. For example, a fairly thin piece of meat like belly or loin pork will need a total curing time of something like one and a half days per 450g (1lb). Thicker pieces like shoulders or legs should be cured for two days per 450g (1lb). So for example, a 4.5kg (10lb) piece of belly or loin of pork will take about 15 days in total, but a leg of the same weight would need 20 days. If you are curing several pieces of meat of differing weights at the same time, take out each piece in turn when its time is up.

What can go wrong

Provided the correct amount of salt is used and the meat is kept cool enough and rubbed each day, dry curing is completely foolproof. However, if at any time the meat grows mould or starts to become slimy, check the temperature and make sure you have used the right amount of salt. If everything seems in order, rub the meat all over with some extra salt, and if possible reduce the temperature, but to no lower than 2°C (36°F).

Finishing the meat

When the meat is fully cured, take it out of the bucket and brush off as much of the spice and unabsorbed salt as you can. Now give it a good wash under the cold tap to remove the last deposits of surface salt. Failure to remove this excess salt could make the meat too dry and salty; it could even make the surface of the meat become damp and slimy, as any surface salt crust will draw moisture out of the air. If this happens, harmful putrefactive mould may grow and spoil all your work.

Once you have washed the meat you should dry it off as

quickly as possible. First, wipe away as much moisture as you can with a *clean* tea towel or piece of muslin. Then, hang the meat in a current of warm air to finish the drying. The traditional way to do this is to hang it up from the ceiling in a warm kitchen. Since my kitchen isn't particularly warm in the winter, when I do most of my curing, I hang up my cured meats in the living room, which is always warm and airy (courtesy of the slow combustion stove). It is important that you don't hang it in cold or stagnant air, as it will be ruined by rampant mould growth. Equally, don't hang it in too warm a place or else the outside will dry out too rapidly, forming a hard skin which moisture deeper inside the meat cannot easily penetrate.

After the curing mixture has done its job, wash off any unabsorbed salt and pieces of spice, then hang the meat up to dry.

You should look at the meat every few days to make sure no excessive mould is developing, although you should expect the appearance of some surface mould – this is to be welcomed, as development of a 'bloom' is a sure sign that the meat is maturing properly. If the mould is anything more than a surface bloom, then you should wipe it away with a dry cloth and be especially vigilant over the next few days. If mould is a problem, then either the meat is in too cold a place or there is insufficient air circulating around the meat, in which case you will have to find a more suitable place for it to hang.

Wherever you decide to hang it, make quite certain that no flies can get to it or your precious meat will be ruined by legions of tunnelling maggots. This is yet another good reason to restrict your curing activities to the winter, when there are (usually) no flies about.

Drying times
The meat may take from a few days to several weeks to dry thoroughly, depending on its size, what animal it was from and exactly where you hang it. When the outside looks thoroughly dry, the drying is complete. You can then cook the meat straight away if you like, or else store it for later use. If you decide to store it, tie it up in a clean pillow case, bury it in a bucket of corn or bran and put it in a cool, dry place, with a piece of muslin tied over the top to keep flies out. It is a good idea to heat the corn or bran in the oven before using it, to kill the mites that are inevitably present, as they also seem to relish the taste of home-cured meat!

You may safely keep the meat for many months in its bucket of bran or corn before cooking it, but remember to use up the small, thin pieces first; these will become dry and leathery sooner than a more susbstantial joint like a big, thick ham. If you don't want to cook a whole piece of meat at once, just cut off what you require and put the rest back.

WET CURING

The wet curing method entails dissolving the curing mixture in water and then steeping the meat to be cured in this sweet, spiced brine. How much brine you need depends on what you are curing and what vessel you are curing in, since obviously, some pieces of meat will pack more compactly into your bucket than others. Consequently, you will have to estimate the amount of brine you need; if you make too little, you can quite easily make up a bit more. If, on the other hand, you make too much, simply store it in bottles in the fridge. Any sort of meat will do for wet curing, but if you decide on a big, thick piece such as a large (weighing more than 5–5.5kg (11–12lb)) leg of pork, then you should dry cure it first for two days by rubbing it with 20g (¾oz) of salt for each 450g (1lb) it weighs. Each day, discard the liquid the salt has drawn out. This dry salting helps drain away excessive juices in the meat which would dilute the brine and encourage the growth of putrefactive mould and bacteria. For pieces of meat under about 4.5kg (10lb) in weight, this initial dry salting should be unnecessary.

Preparing the brine
First of all estimate the quantity of brine needed to cover the meat by at least 5cm (2"). Put the appropriate quantity of water in a large pan and bring to the boil. When the water boils, turn the heat down and simmer gently for ten minutes with the pan uncovered. Boiling not only ensures the water is sterile, but also helps to remove any hardness in the water and drives away the chlorine put in by the Water Board, both of which are harmful to the meat.

While the water is simmering, crush (*not* grind) the spices by tying them up securely in a clean tea towel and bashing them with a rolling pin or wooden mallet. If you are using herbs, simply chop them up coarsely with scissors or a sharp knife. You should use the same sort of spices and herbs you would use for dry curing, allowing 60g (2oz) or so of spice per 4.5 litres (1 gallon) of brine. If you want to use herbs instead or as well, then use two handfuls of fresh herbs or 45g (1½oz) of dried herbs per 4.5 litres of brine. Tie the spice and any herbs securely in a little bag made from a square of muslin.

After the water has simmered for ten minutes, remove the pan from the heat and dissolve the sugar and salt in it. You should allow 1kg (2¼lb) of salt and 225g (8oz) of sugar per 4.5 litres (1 gallon) of water. When dissolved, drop in the bag of spice, cover with a lid, and leave to go cold. When nearly cold, add the ascorbic acid – if you are using it – and give the solution a good stir. If you *do* decide to use ascorbic acid, you will need to use rather more than for dry curing. You should use 4g (⅛oz) for every 4.5kg (10lb) of meat, and in addition to that add 5g (⅙oz) for every 4.5 litres of water you use. So for example, a 4.5kg ham cured in a brine made with 9 litres (2 gallons) of water, will need 14g (½oz) of ascorbic acid. Remember, though, that if you are using a dark sugar or molasses the meat will also be quite dark, so there is no point adding ascorbic acid.

The brine must now be chilled to between 2 and 4°C (36–39°F). When it has reached this temperature, put the meat into your curing bucket and cover it with the chilled brine. You will find the meat has a marked tendency to float, so you will have to devise some way of keeping it covered by at least 5cm (2″) of brine. The lid of the curing bucket or a big dinner plate weighed down with a large *clean* stone is very effective. Never use a metallic object, as it would be rapidly corroded by the salt.

Overhauling

As the curing progresses, the meat absorbs salt from the brine and so the brine becomes weaker. If this is not counteracted by adding more salt, the brine will become so weak that harmful bacteria will be able to grow in it and the meat will be ruined. For this reason it is essential to maintain an adequate level of salt in the solution. The traditional way of checking the salt level is by floating an egg or potato in the brine. If the egg or potato floats nice and high in the brine, the brine contains enough salt. If not, it must be strengthened by dissolving more salt in it. Since the traditional potato or egg method is rather hit or miss, a much better way is to use a winemaker's hydrometer – which is, after all, really only a more refined version of the egg/potato method. This process of checking and adjusting the strength of the brine is called *overhauling*.

You should overhaul every three or four days. On each occasion, first take the meat out of the bucket and then give the brine a good stir. Now float the hydrometer in it and take a reading. If the reading is below 1.155, the brine will have to be strengthened. For every four degrees it is under strength you must add 30g (1oz) of salt per 4.5 litres (1 gallon) of brine; determining how much brine you have in your bucket is very easy if it is calibrated. So for example, if 9 litres (2 gallons) of brine had a strength of 1.143, then it would be 1.155–1.143 =12 degrees under strength. So in this case, adding 30g of salt per 4.5 litres of brine *for every 4 degrees under strength* would mean adding 90g (3oz) of salt for each 4.5 litres of brine. Since there are 9 litres of brine, this means a total of 180g (6oz) of salt must be added.

Having worked out how much salt to use, add it to the brine and stir well to ensure it is completely dissolved. Now return the meat to the bucket and allow the curing process to continue.

How long to cure

The meat should be left in the cure for a total of three to four days per 450g (1lb) for large, thick pieces like legs and shoulders, and for about half that time for the thinner cuts. Also bear in mind that lean meat cures faster than fatty meat. If you are curing several pieces of meat of different weights, remove each piece in turn when its time is up. When a piece of meat is fully cured, take it out of the brine and then wash, dry and store it as you would dry cured meat – see Dry Curing above.

Possible problems

Should mould appear on the surface of the brine at any time during curing, skim it off at once, give the brine a good stir and check the salt level with the hydrometer, adding more salt if the reading is below 1.155. You should also check the temperature of the brine and if necessary turn the fridge up to a cooler setting. Should the brine at any time become thick and viscous – or 'ropy', as this condition is known – then harmful bacteria are proliferating and *immediate* action is required. First take the meat out of the brine and scrub it well under the cold tap. Now discard the brine and wash out the bucket with very hot soapy water, remembering to rinse away all traces of soap. Return the meat to the bucket, and refill with fresh, chilled brine. Over the next few days, keep an especially close eye on it for signs of further trouble. Fortunately, you are only likely to encounter these problems if you don't keep the meat cool enough or if you let the salt level fall too low.

Storing the brine

Once you have finished curing, you can quite safely keep your brine until the next time – but only if you ensure that it contains sufficient salt, and is kept cold. Test and restrengthen if necessary, and keep it at the curing temperature of between 2 and 4°C (36–39°F). Before storing, strain it through a fine sieve into clean glass or food-grade plastic bottles, and seal tightly with salt-proof lids or stoppers.

MAKING CORNED BEEF

Making your own corned beef is a real money saver, and it tastes far nicer than the ghastly pink stuff that comes in cans.

Choose a nice cheap cut of beef such as rolled brisket – a piece 1.35–1.8kg (3–4lb) in weight is ideal. Weigh the meat

and make up a dry curing mixture using 90g (3oz) of salt
and 30g (1oz) of sugar (white or brown) for every 1.35kg of
meat. Rub the cure into the meat and leave for 24 hours. In
the meantime, make up in the usual way enough wet curing
solution to cover the meat by 5cm (2") or so, allowing 1kg
(2¼lb) of salt and 450g (1lb) of sugar (white or brown) per
4.5 litres (1 gallon) of water. You can use whatever spices
and herbs you fancy, and if you want the beef to have a
rosier colour, remember to use some ascorbic acid. When the
brine has been chilled, dissolve in it 15g (½oz) of sodium
bicarbonate for every 4.5 litres.

After the meat has been dry salted, transfer it to the
curing solution and cure for one week for every 450g weight,
remembering to overhaul it every three days, adjusting salt
levels as necessary. Once cured, it is a good idea to cook the
meat straight away, as cured beef tends to become rather
dry if stored for any length of time.

LIGHT CURING

If you intend to cook your cured meats as soon as they are
ready rather than store them for a while, then it is possible
to cure using rather less salt to produce meats which are less
salty and more succulent – although lacking the true cured
flavour. To do this using the dry method, simply put half the
amount of salt in the cure but otherwise continue as usual.
If you are using the wet method, make a standard strength
brine but halve the curing time.

Always remember that lightly cured meats won't keep,
and must be cooked and eaten almost immediately. They
should be kept refrigerated at all times.

COOKING AND STORING CURED MEATS

Always store your cured meats out of strong light, as this
can make the fat turn rancid. As well as being unpleasant,
rancid fat is also a health hazard.

When the time comes to cook your meat, you should first
wash off any surface mould or bloom with warm water. Then
you should soak the meat in cold water before cooking it, to
draw out some of the salt which has done its job as
preservative and can now be dispensed with.

Small, thin pieces of meat will only need a few hours'
soaking, whereas large hams may need up to several days.

When soaking larger pieces, remember to change the water every twelve hours, or the salt won't be drawn out of the meat effectively.

A word of caution: don't soak slices of bacon unless you have used too much salt in the curing and they really are too salty to be enjoyed as they are. If this is the case, soak them for no more than ten minutes or the bacon will be tasteless. And whatever the meat, never oversoak it; this extracts not only the salt, but the flavour as well. Meats that are only lightly cured contain much less salt, so don't need to be soaked before cooking.

Having soaked excess salt out of the meat, a good way to cook it is to simmer it gently in a pan of water with some chopped-up vegetables and herbs of your choice; allow approximately 20 minutes for every 450g (1lb) plus an extra 20 minutes. When cooked, leave the meat to cool in the liquid before removing it.

Another way to cook your meat, and the best way to cook corned beef, is to roast it in a covered dish in the oven at 160°C (325°F), gas mark 3, allowing 45 minutes per 450g (1lb). When cooked, remove from the oven and leave the meat to cool in the dish. The following day the meat will have set firmly and can be cut into thin slices and served. Some cured meats, notably bacon, can equally well be sliced thinly and grilled or fried instead.

5.
JAM MAKING

Without the use of copious quantities of white sugar it would be quite impossible to make conventional jams. Such jams rely heavily on the sugar to act as a preservative, and for this to be effective they must contain something like 60 per cent sugar. Any food that contains this amount of sugar, as most supermarket jams do, can hardly be called healthy; even the sugar companies admit that sugary foods will rot your teeth, and many food experts go further and condemn excessive sugar consumption as a very serious general health hazard. Eminent nutritionists like Professor John Yudkin have linked sugar consumption with increased risk of degenerative diseases like diabetes and heart disease. Excessive sugar consumption may even be responsible, directly or indirectly, for some types of cancer.

Much of the sugar we consume each year is in an 'invisible' form, by which I mean that we buy it not as bags of sugar as such, but as an ingredient of many modern processed foods. This means that even if you don't buy sugar as a separate item at all – but have an otherwise fairly typical British diet – you will still be consuming considerable quantities of a substance that is, in excess, potentially deadly; most people munch their way through nearly a hundred-weight of the stuff every year! If this seems rather a lot, remember that if you eat much processed food, then your sugar intake may be very much more than you realize – a closer look at the ingredients of your favourite foods will soon convince you of this. In view of this, it would be wise for us all to play safe and reduce our sugar consumption wherever possible. This was very much the message of the much vaunted NACNE report, which recommends that we should cut our present sugar consumption by half. A good start can be made but cutting out ordinary high-sugar jams and eating no-sugar jams instead.

Yet another health hazard of ordinary supermarket jams is the presence of the ubiquitous additives, especially artificial colourings and preservatives. The colourings in jam are especially worrying, as they are all too often synthetic, coal-tar derived 'azo' dyes. These azo dyes have been shown to cause hyperactivity in children, as well as various forms of intolerance (i.e. allergic) reactions, especially in people who react badly to aspirin.

JAMS MADE WITHOUT SUGAR

You *can* avoid both the sugar and the additives if you buy one of the many brands of sugarless jams from Health Food shops – but at a price. These jams really are quite expensive – something over three times the price of ordinary jams. Instead of using sugar as a preservative, these jams keep because they are sterilized by heat, and are then hermetically sealed in their jars, so preventing the ingress of moulds and other bugs that would make the jam go bad. Once opened, these jams must be either eaten within a few days, or else stored in a refrigerator.

Happily, you can easily make your own sugar-free jams which are every bit as good as the health-shop offerings but cheaper to make than the price of a jar of the high-sugar kind sold at the local supermarket. There is, however, one technical snag to not using sugar in your jams, namely that they might not set solid like their high-sugar counterparts. Ordinary jams set because the large amount of sugar present reacts with pectin and acid in the fruit to form a solid gel. The absence or weakness of set in sugar-free jams is for all practical purposes totally unimportant. What *is* important is the flavour of the jam, and since jams made without sugar are not overpoweringly sweet, and contain a much higher proportion of fruit, they have an incomparably superior flavour to that of ordinary jam. Another advantage of no-sugar jams is that they don't require long cooking times, and consequently have a much fresher, fruitier flavour, unlike conventional jams which require protracted boiling. A weaker set seems a small price to pay for all this extra quality.

Even though the jams described in this chapter do tend to have quite weak sets, sometimes you will be surprised to find that you have a really firm set for no apparent reason. This variability in set is due to the natural variations in the amounts of pectin, acids and sugars in the fruit. Even the professional manufacturers of no-sugar jams seem to have trouble making their jams set consistently, judging by the way a given brand and type of jam can sometimes be set almost solid and yet at other times can be quite runny. The variability in the setting quality of sugar-free jams is something you very quickly get used to, in exactly the same way that you get used to home-cured ham produced without dangerous nitrates and nitrites looking grey or tan, rather than bright pink like the supermarket kind, or homemade sausage not looking a similar puce shade of pink. And if you simply *must* have jam with a definite firm set, then you can use agar powder (more correctly, agar agar, a seaweed derivative with similar properties to gelatine) to produce it.

JAM MAKING IN PRACTICE

Choice of fruit

The beauty of sugar-free jam is that you don't have to worry about how much pectin your fruit contains, since a firm set isn't essential to its success. This means you can use whatever type of fruit you like; the main consideration is how it tastes. However, fruits that do usually contain plenty of pectin – gooseberries and blackcurrants, for instance – are more likely to produce a jam that sets without the need to use agar. So if you are keen to produce a jam with a pectin set, you should stick to the fruits in the table below, and ensure that the fruit is not overripe, as overripe fruit contains much less pectin.

High-Pectin Fruits
Cooking Apples
Crab Apples
Gooseberries
Most Plums
Redcurrants
Blackcurrants
Damsons

Even if you do use high-pectin fruits, there is no guarantee that the jam will set as firmly as you would like; the only *certain* way is to use agar. Another prerequisite for a natural pectin set is acid; if the fruit doesn't contain enough, then you greatly reduce your chance of getting a good set. Fruit low in natural acid, such as strawberries, peaches and some cherries, should have it added in the form of lemon juice: use the juice from one lemon for each 1.35kg (3lb) of fruit.

Very acidic fruits, on the other hand, like rhubarb (which is really a vegetable, of course), are not good candidates for the no-sugar method of jam making, since you would need to use an awful lot of sweetener to mask the sharpness, so rather defeating the object of using a low-sugar recipe. If you do fancy making some low-sugar rhubarb jam, use half sweet apples and half rhubarb.

Choice of Sweetener

Most of our British fruits, unless exceptionally ripe, do tend to taste rather tart because of their relatively high acid content. So, since a firm set is not of paramount importance, the principle role of a sweetener is to offset this sharpness slightly, making the jam more palatable. The best sweetener to use is honey, since no other sweetener blends so harmoniously with the subtle, delicate flavours of fruits. Having said that, you *could* use one of the genuine brown sugars (genuine brown sugars have a country of origin marked on the packet), or even white sugar, though I wouldn't use these myself. Because the sweetener only serves to offset the tartness of the fruit, how little or much you use is entirely your decision, and in the recipes that follow, no specific amounts are stipulated. Always remember, though, that honey consists largely of sugars, and so is probably little better than sugar from a health point of view.

Equipment for Jam Making

The main item of equipment you will need is a pan to cook the jam in, and this must be big enough to handle the largest quantity of jam you want to make at any one time. A large saucepan would probably fit the bill perfectly, although if you intend to make sizeable amounts, a proper preserving pan would be better. For all the recipes given below, a pan with a capacity of about 4.5 litres (8 pints) will be ample. Remember when choosing a pan that you won't want to have it more than about half full, or else jam will splash out all over the stove.

If at all possible, use a stainless steel pan; but if you don't have, or can't afford, one of these, then an aluminium pan will do. The only trouble with aluminium is that it is attacked by the acids in the jam, and this results in potentially harmful aluminium salts being leached into the jam. Some people definitely are allergic to aluminium, but most of us seem to be immune. I use a traditional brass jam pan, even though the copper in it tends to reduce the vitamin C content of the jam slightly. Copper or brass jam pans do have an advantage in that they give gooseberry jam an attractive green colour; even so, stainless steel pans are preferable, and if this book sells well, I'll buy myself one! Whatever sort of pan you use, make sure it isn't made of iron, or the jam will acquire a horrible metallic taste from it. If possible, choose a pan with a nice thick bottom, as this will spread the heat more evenly and prevent the jam from sticking.

You will also need a supply of ½ litre (450g/1lb) hermetic fruit preserving jars – the kilner type are excellent – and a second pan to sterilize the jars in. Since all the recipes in this chapter make about 1.8kg (4lb) of jam, the sterilizing pan must be big enough to hold at least four ½ litre jars. You will also need some sort of trivet to prevent the jars of jam coming into direct contact with the bottom of the pan. If you haven't got a proper trivet, a thick, folded dish-cloth will suffice. Bear in mind that there must be enough room above the jars to allow a lid to be fitted. If you haven't got a lid for the pan, a thick, close-weave cloth draped over the top will do instead.

Finally, you will need a measuring jug, a jam funnel, a potato masher and a long-handled wooden spoon to stir the jam with. The longer the handle, the less likely you are to get splashed by flying dollops of boiling jam.

GENERAL METHOD

First of all the fruit should be washed and allowed to drain for a few minutes. Next, any stalks and other unwanted matter should be removed. Fruits with large stones, like plums and peaches, should be cut in half and their stones removed. Having washed and prepared the fruit, you should chop large fruit roughly into chunks; smaller fruits like currants and berries can be left whole. Dump the prepared fruit into your pan and add the amount of water indicated in the recipe. *Very gently* begin heating the pan, stirring the fruit about to prevent it from burning. Once the fruit softens and begins to go mushy, help it along by mashing it well with the potato masher. Simmer gently until you have a nice mush; most fruits will get to this stage within about 30 to 40 minutes.

You should now sweeten the jam with just enough honey (or sugar) to make the jam palatable, but before adding it, remove the pan from the heat. How much you use is up to you, but don't overdo it. Remember to stir in each addition of honey until completely dissolved, and then taste the jam before deciding whether to add any more.

Using agar
If you are going to use agar to ensure the jam sets firmly, this should be added at the same time as you add the honey or sugar. To work out how much agar to add, you must first know how much jam you have in your pan; a pan graduated internally is a great asset here. If your pan isn't so marked, you will have to measure out the jam into a bowl using a measuring jug, and then return it to the pan afterwards. For each 870ml (1½ pints) of jam, you must allow 2 level tsp of agar powder. The agar powder should be prepared before adding it to the jam by putting it into a small bowl or cup, and adding one tbs of *cold* water for each tsp of agar. Stir well, and leave the agar to soak for at least ten minutes. When the agar has soaked sufficiently, quickly stir it into the jam and return the pan to the heat, then bring it to the boil stirring continuously. Boil vigorously for three minutes, then take the pan off the heat and allow the jam to cool for five minutes before potting.

Potting the jam
The jars should be scrupulously clean, and should be heated in a cool oven, 107°C (225°F), gas mark ¼, for at least half an hour before use. Fill the jars to within 1cm (½") of the top and put the lids on immediately, remembering to use the rubber sealing rings. If you are using jars that have plastic screw bands (such as the kilner type), screw the bands down tight, and then slacken them off a quarter turn. If you are using jars with metal clip type sealing devices, engage the two parts of the clip to hold the lid down loosely, but don't

Once the jam has been sweetened, fill the preheated jars with jam using a heatproof jug and a jam funnel.

pull the levers down yet. Stand the jars on a trivet or folded cloth in the pan you intend to sterilize them in, and fill it with hot water so that the water comes up to about 2½ cm (1″) below the tops of the jars. Put the lid on the pan, bring the water quickly to simmering point and simmer for 35 minutes.

At the end of this time, remove the jars from the pan and immediately clip or screw the lids down tightly. Leave the jars in a draught-free place until cold, and then store in a cool, dark place until needed. It is a good idea to keep your jam for a couple of weeks before you start eating it, as it definitely seems to improve for a little keeping. Unopened, the jam will keep almost indefinitely, but once opened, the jam should if possible be stored in a fridge or cold larder. In a fridge, it should remain sound for a couple of weeks at least.

RECIPES

Peach jam

2kg (4½lb) ripe peaches
juice of a large lemon
120ml (4floz) water
honey or sugar
agar powder (optional)

Remove any stalks from the peaches, then wash them. Stone the peaches by cutting through to the stone with a very sharp knife all the way round following the crease. Give the halves a sharp twist in opposite directions; the halves of the peach should then separate fairly cleanly, leaving the stone in one half. The stone can now be carefully scooped out with a spoon.

Chop the peaches into small chunks and place in your pan, together with the lemon juice and water. Heat the pan *very gently* until the juice runs freely, then mash the peaches with a potato masher. Simmer until very mushy. Sweeten with honey or sugar to taste, and if used, add the agar – see general method. Boil rapidly for three minutes, leave to cool for five minutes, then pot and sterilize as described on page 77.

When you have potted the jam, you may find it tends to separate, leaving the juice below as the fruit rises slightly. If this happens, allow to cool until the jam thickens, and then give the jars a shake to re-homogenize it.

Yield about: 1.8kg (4lb).

Plum jam

2kg (4½lb) sweet plums
90ml (3floz) water
honey or sugar
agar (optional)

Wash the plums and remove any stalks. Cut them in half and remove the stones. Chop roughly and place in the pan with the water. Cook gently for about 30 minutes until mushy, giving the plums an occasional mash with the potato masher. Sweeten with honey or sugar to taste, and if used, add the agar. Boil rapidly for three minutes then pot and sterilize (see page 77).

Yield: about 1.8kg (4lb).

Blackcurrant jam

1.8kg (4lb) blackcurrants
150ml (5floz) water
honey or sugar
agar (optional)

Remove the stalks from the currants. Wash and drain well, then place in your pan with the water. Heat gently and cook for about thirty minutes until soft, mashing occasionally.

Sweeten to taste and add the agar – if you're using it. Boil for three minutes then pot and sterilize as usual (see page 77).

You can use white or redcurrants instead of the blackcurrants, or a mixture of any two, or even all three.

Yield: about 1.8kg (4lb).

Gooseberry jam

1.8kg (4lb) gooseberries
180ml (6floz) water
honey or sugar
agar (optional)

Top and tail the gooseberries, then wash and drain well. Cook slowly with the water for 40 minutes until mushy, stirring continuously. When soft enough to do so, mash them well with the potato masher. Add the honey and, if you're using it, the agar. Boil rapidly for three minutes. Pot and sterilize in the usual way (see page 77).

To make this jam even more tastier, remove the flowers from eight large elderflower heads; avoid as much green stalk as possible. Tie them up in a muslin bag and place into the pan as soon as possible after the juice begins to run, removing immediately before potting. Elderflowers impart a delicious muscat flavour to the jam.

Yield: about 1.8kg (4lb).

Damson jam

2kg (4½lb) large damsons
90ml (3floz) water
honey or sugar
agar (optional)

Remove any stalks from the damsons and then wash and drain them well. Cut the damsons in half and remove the stones; this can be a bit fiddly sometimes, but well worth it for this delicious jam.

Put the stoned damsons and water into the pan and cook gently for about half an hour until the damsons are soft and mushy, giving them an occasional mash to help things along.

When nice and pulpy, sweeten to taste and add any agar. Boil rapidly for three minutes before potting and sterilizing in the usual way (see page 77).

Yield: about 1.8kg (4lb).

6.
SOFT CHEESE

Low-fat cottage and curd cheeses are very popular with health-conscious people these days, but ironically, the supermarket versions of these 'healthier' cheeses are often full of additives, typically in the guise of stabilizers and emulsifiers. These are used to prevent the cheese separating into curds and whey, which it tends to do because the considerable time delay between manufacture and eventual consumption – really fresh cheese doesn't need these things. Although it is possible to buy some types of soft cheeses that are free of dubious additives, they are not stocked everywhere, and you may have to shop around a bit.

Having made my own cheeses now for many years, I always find commercially made soft cheeses rather bland compared with the ones I make myself. Making your own affords you complete control over the flavour and texture of the finished product, and since soft cheese will keep well in a deep freeze for at least six months, it is very easy to be completely self-sufficient in your favourite cheeses even if you only make cheese twice a year.

PRINCIPLES OF CHEESEMAKING

Cheesemaking is really only a clever way of concentrating the solid, nutritious part of milk and persuading the watery part (the whey) to drain off. There are basically two methods you can use to achieve this result, and both rely on the ability of the milk solids to coagulate under certain special circumstances. The first method is to raise the acidity of the milk to such a level that the proteins in it start to bind together to form solid curds. This phenomenon can be seen when you pour milk onto stewed rhubarb or other acidic fruit. You can actually make a soft cheese in this way by adding lemon or other citrus fruit juice to warm milk and then straining off the curds through a piece of muslin. The trouble with cheese made by this method is that it tastes rather bland, although it is useful for cooking.

A better, more flavoursome way of increasing the acidity of the milk is to enlist the help of natural bacteria which ferment the lactose in the milk into lactic acid. Cheese made by the action of these lactic acid bacteria are called *lactic* cheeses. They are much more flavoursome, and usually have a pleasant acidic bite to them. In fresh raw milk, these lactic acid bacteria occur naturally. Sadly, most of us can only get the cooked sort in which the pasteurization or sterilization process has killed off these beneficial bugs, and so we will have to reintroduce them specially. This isn't as difficult as it may sound, since the necessary bacteria are readily available in little packets of freeze-dried cheese culture. Many healthfood shops now stock cheese starter culture, but if yours doesn't, see page 158 for the name and address of a mail order supplier.

Rennet

The other way you can persuade the milk solids to coagulate is by the action of a special enzymic preparation called *rennet*. Rennet is made from an extract of the stomach of calves, and so is a perfectly natural and traditional aid to your cheesemaking. Proper cheesemaking rennet is quite easy to procure, but you will have to send off for it as it is most unlikely that any of your local shops will stock it. What you *will* be able to get locally is rennet intended for junket making; this is quite suitable for making soft cheese, although not as cheap to use as cheesemaking rennet. Cheeses made with rennet are much firmer in texture than the lactic kind, and this is why rennet is usually used to make cottage cheese. Cheeses made only with rennet are once again rather bland, so often rennet and lactic acid bacteria are used together to produce a cheese of the desired blend of texture and flavour.

Milk for cheesemaking

Milk from all sorts of animals including sheep and buffalo is used for cheesemaking, and even in Britain, cheeses made with ewes milk are gradually becoming popular. Most of us though, will only have the choice between goats' and cows' milk, and of the two, the more economical choice will be cows'. You can equally well use pasteurized, sterilized or, if you can get it, raw milk, and the flavour and texture of the cheese to some extent depends on whether the milk has been heat treated or not. If you want to make a low fat cheese, you should use skimmed milk.

Equipment for cheesemaking

To make soft cheese you will need a colander (preferably a stainless steel one), a thermometer and two 45cm (18″) squares of fine weave muslin, or cheesecloth. You will also need a saucepan large enough to heat up to 2.3 litres (4pt) of milk in. This too should ideally be made of stainless steel, but aluminium will do. It must not be made of iron, brass or copper, but an iron pan with an enamelled interior is quite suitable, provided the interior enamelling is completely undamaged. A one litre vacuum flask is also very useful, but not essential.

MAKING LACTIC CHEESE

Preparing the Starter

Before you can make your first batch of lactic cheese, you will have to prepare a special culture of the lactic acid bacteria known as a *starter*. To make this you will need 1 litre (2pt) of milk and a packet of cheese culture bought from either a health food shop or a specialist supplier (see page 158). One sachet will usually make about 1 litre (2pt) of starter.

First heat the milk to boiling point, then cool it as rapidly as possible to 22°C (72°F) (unless the instructions on the packet stipulate a different temperature) by standing the pan in a sink of cold water. While the milk is cooling, mix the contents of the sachet to a thin paste with a little water in a *clean* teacup, making sure you get out any lumps. When the milk has cooled sufficiently, stir the paste into the milk, stirring thoroughly to ensure it is evenly distributed, then put the lid on the pan. You must now keep the inoculated milk at as near as possible 22°C (or the temperature indicated on the packet) for between twelve and twenty four hours – make absolutely sure you don't overheat it or you will kill the bacteria. A good way of keeping the milk warm is to put the pan near a radiator or stove, or even in an airing cupboard. A simpler solution, I find, is to pour the starter into a vaccum flask; that way you don't have to worry about whether the milk is too hot or too cold, since the insulating properties of the flask will guarantee that the starter will be maintained at the correct temperature. If you do use a flask, remember to pre heat it first with some hot water, or the starter will be cooled excessively when you pour it in.

After about twelve hours' incubation, take a look at the starter and smell it. If it has started to get thick and smells distinctly cheesy, then it is ready; if not, leave it a little longer.

Once the starter is ready, you can make your first batch of cheese from it. But if you have a deep freeze, a better plan is to freeze the starter in small amounts and use these to inoculate further batches of milk, from which you will then make your cheese. The great advantage in this latter course of action is that you will be able to make far more cheese from your packet of culture, and the cheese will be of a much better quality.

If you don't have a deep freeze or you want to make the first batch of cheese from the starter, proceed as follows. Pour the starter into a saucepan and *slowly* heat it to 32°C (90°F), stirring gently all the time. If you want to make a second batch of cheese, then before heating the starter put 2 tablespoons of it in a sealed jar and keep it in the fridge until needed. Provided it is kept cool, it should keep for up to a week.

While the milk is being heated, line the colander with muslin and stand it on the draining board of your sink. Once the starter reaches 32°C, pour it into the colander and allow it to drain, keeping the colander well covered with the other square of muslin. You should give the cheese a stir from time to time to aid rapid draining. As soon as most of the whey has drained, gather together the four corners of the cloth and tie them together with a piece of string. Now hang the cheese up to continue draining. Every so often you should untie the cloth and scrape the cheese down off the sides and mix it in with the rest. Allow the cheese to continue draining until it has a nice firm texture.

Provided the cheese is made in a reasonably warm room, the total draining time should only be a few hours. If the room is cold, the cheese won't drain properly and the draining may take a day or more to complete.

Flavouring the cheese

To add extra flavour you can mix in a little salt with the drained cheese, or better still use finely chopped olives, vegetables, fruits, nuts, herbs or whatever you fancy.

Subsequent batches

To make a second batch of cheese, use the starter saved from the first batch to inoculate the milk in place of the sachet of dried culture, but otherwise continue exactly as before.

Once you have made your second batch of cheese you can again save 2 tablespoons of it to inoculate the milk for the third batch, and so on. Unfortunately, you won't be able to carry on doing this indefinitely, since as the culture is saved and reused it very soon weakens and becomes contaminated with undesirable organisms. When this happens, the cheese will start to develop off-flavours and so you will have to buy another packet of dried culture and start again.

Freezing the starter

If, instead of using the starter to make cheese, you freeze it and then use the frozen starter to inoculate the milk, you won't have to put up with cheese that diminishes in quality as the saved culture weakens and becomes contaminated. You will also be able to make far more cheese per packet of culture.

The best way to freeze starter is in little glass lemonade bottles. Assuming you intend making cheese using 1 litre (2pt) milk each time, you should put 2 tablespoons of starter in each bottle. If you want to make cheese on a larger scale, put proportionately more in each bottle, allowing 1 tablespoon of starter per ½ litre (1pt) milk. Always freeze the bottles on their sides, and never more than half-fill them or they may crack when they are frozen. If you haven't got room in your deep freeze for bottles, an alternative is to freeze the starter in ice-cube trays. This method isn't quite so good, as the culture tends to dehydrate and weaken; to minimize this, put the tray of starter in a polythene bag as soon as it is frozen and seal tightly. Before using frozen starter to inoculate the milk, allow it to thaw gently. Using your initial starter in this way will allow you to make up to 7.2kg (16lb) of cheese from one packet of dried culture.

COTTAGE CHEESE

This is one of the most popular soft cheeses, but it is a little more tricky to make than the lactic kind. Traditionally it is made using skimmed milk, but you can equally well use whole milk if you fancy a bit of extra creaminess. As with lactic cheese, you will need to have some starter ready beforehand; if you haven't made any yet, see the section on preparing starter above.

Take 2 litres (4pt) of milk, bring to the boil and cool immediately to 30°C (85°F), then stir in 2 tablespoons of starter. Immediately you have added the starter, stir in 3 teaspoons of junket rennet (or ¼ teaspoon of proper cheesemaking rennet) which has first been diluted in 1 tablespoon of cold water. Stir the milk thoroughly for about a minute, cover the pan and leave in a warm place overnight.

In the morning there should be a solid white curd which may have shrunk away from the sides of the pan slightly revealing the greenish whey. Cut the curd up into 1cm (½") pieces using a long-bladed knife as shown in the illustration below. You should now *very slowly* heat the curds and whey to 57°C (135°F), taking about half an hour to do so. While it

When the milk has formed a solid curd, using a sharp knife, cut it first into slabs, then cut at right angles to form square columns. Finally, with the blade of the knife inclined to the surface of the curd, cut the columns into small pieces.

is heating up, stir the pieces of curd from time to time to
help them drain and prevent them sticking together; take
great care to do this gently, or the curd will be broken up
and the texture of the cheese spoiled.

As soon as the temperature reaches 57°C (135°F), pour the
curds and whey into a colander lined with muslin or cheesecloth and allow to drain. Remember to keep the cheese in a
warm place or it won't drain properly, and remember also to
stir it gently from time to time to prevent it sticking
together in one lump. You should allow the cheese to drain
until most of the whey has run off and the cheese has taken
on the characteristically firm cottage cheese texture.
Because cottage cheese has a much coarser texture than
lactic cheese, it drains very much more quickly, and with
luck should be completely drained within an hour.

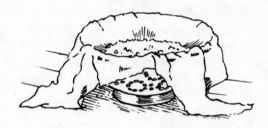

Once the cheese has drained sufficiently, turn it out of the
cloth into a bowl. If you want to, you can add a little salt or
some chopped herbs, or fruit, vegetables or nuts to it.
Whether or not you add anything to your cheese, you should
now give it a gentle stir to break it up slightly. Don't overdo
this or you will break the cheese into crumbs and so spoil its
nice coarse texture. The cheese is now ready to eat.

MAKING QUESO BLANCO

This is a quickly and easily made Latin-American cheese
which is suitable for use in cooking or just eating as it is
with fruit or as part of a salad. Instead of using the starter
or rennet to coagulate the milk, lemon juice is used; this
gives the cheese a rather unusual lemony flavour. If you
prefer, the juice of other citrus fruits can be used instead.

To make queso blanco, first bring 1 litre (2pt) milk to the boil and then cool immediately to 77°C (170°F). Stir in 150ml (¼pt) of freshly squeezed lemon juice (approximately the juice of 2 lemons). You should see the milk curdle immediately; keep stirring for a few seconds, then let the curds and whey rest for a few minutes before pouring the whole lot into a muslin-lined colander. Leave to drain in a warm place until most of the whey has drained off – this should only take a few minutes. Traditionally, queso blanco is heavily salted, but you don't have to add any at all if you prefer not to.

Strictly speaking, to make proper queso blanco you should now pack the cheese into some sort of mould and press it with a heavy weight. You can have a go at this if you feel inclined, but the cheese is quite delicious as it is, and can be used in the same way as you would cottage cheese.

STORING SOFT CHEESES

Soft cheeses will keep well for about a week or so in a cool place such as a fridge. If you add chopped fruits, vegetables or other ingredients to it it won't keep quite so long. For long-term storage it should be kept in a deep freeze, where it should store well for at least six months.

7.
PIES, PATES AND TERRINES

Like sausages and burgers, pork and other meat pies are a rubbish bin for the meat industry. For example, in Britain the legal minimum meat content of a pork pie is only 25 per cent, and remember meat isn't the same thing as lean meat. British regulations require that only 50 per cent of the 'meat' has to be 'lean meat', so the minimum quantity of real meat in a British pork pie can be a mere 12.5 per cent. What of the other 12.5 per cent of 'meat'? Well, this can include fat, skin, gristle, sinew, pancreas, diaphragm and thymus. Even the 'lean meat' isn't necessarily what it seems, since Mechanically Recovered Meat (MRM – see chapter 3 for details) can legally be included in the lean meat content of pies and other meat products, and the manufacturer doesn't even have to tell you about it on the label. In the USA there are restrictions on its use and a requirement that when MRM is used it must be declared on the list of ingredients.

So much for the 'meat' half of your pork pie. The other 50 per cent of a pork pie is made up of the pastry case, various cereal extenders to spin out the token meat content even further, lots of fat and, of course, the usual assortment of additives. And since a pork pie is a cooked meat product, other slaughter house scraps can go into it, including things like brains, feet, lungs, oesophaguses, rectums, spinal cords, udders and testicles. For all this, fat is really the key ingredient in these products as far as danger to health is concerned. Fat is cheap and plentiful, and there are no regulations limiting the amount that can be used. The industry takes full advantage of this, not only with meat pies, but with just about every other meat product it makes, including sausages and patés. As an experiment, I devised a recipe for a pork pie that would just conform to the minimum meat content required by the regulations. The result was a pie that contained nearly 50 per cent fat! Now if *I* can easily devise such a pie in my own kitchen, think how much better the meat industry can do with its legions of food technologists, chemists and high-tech machines. Just how much fat their pies contain, I dread to think.

HOMEMADE PORK AND GAME PIES

To make a proper pork or game pie you will have to master the art of making a pastry case that will stand up on its own without any support. To make one of these you need to use a special type of pastry called hot water pastry. This is made from a mixture of flour, hot milk and melted fat which you work together into a soft paste. This paste is then formed into the pie case, using your fingers to gently raise the pastry to make the sides of the pie. This is why these traditional types of pie are called 'hand raised'.

Once you've made the case – or crust, to give it its proper name – you then fill it with the chopped and seasoned meat, and seal it with a lid made from a little pastry put aside; the pie is then ready to bake.

RECIPES

Melton Mowbray pie
The crowned king of pork pies is the Melton Mowbray pie – not to be confused with the hideous imitations made by the well-known commercial pork pie manufacturers. The first Melton Mowbray pies were probably made in the fourteenth century, and for centuries these pies were served as part of a high tea to hungry fox hunters on their return from their afternoon's 'sport'. Whatever you think about fox hunting, these pies are truly magnificent.

To make a Melton Mowbray pie, you must use only good quality lean pork, and it must be *chopped* into ½cm (¼") cubes using a very sharp knife. Although this sounds laborious, it is the only way to make a genuine Melton Mowbray pie. If you mince the meat or use other similar mechanical aids such as food processors, you will spoil the texture of the meat and ruin the character of the pie.

Pastry crust

900g (2lb) wholemeal flour
400g (14oz) butter
55g (2oz) suet
290ml (½pt) milk
½ teaspoon salt
1 beaten egg for glazing

Filling

1.35kg (3lb) pork*
1½ teaspoons ground black pepper
*2 tablespoons finely chopped fresh sage – use the same
    amount of dried if you haven't any fresh*
1 teaspoon ground mace

*The best cuts of pork to use are leg and shoulder; all skin and gristle must be removed, but a little fat can be included. Don't throw away the skin and gristle – save it for the jelly.

Jelly

1.2 litres (2pt) water
2 medium-sized onions
4 bay leaves
1 teaspoon freshly ground black pepper
pork bones, skin and gristle – see method below
*2 teaspoons each of finely chopped fresh sage, marjoram and
    thyme – alternatively, use the same amount of dried herbs*
gelatine – see method below

Preparing the jelly

Much of the character of this pie depends on the highly flavoured jellified stock that is poured into the pie after it is cooked, in order to fill any gaps between the filling and the crust.

The jelly should be prepared the day before you intend to make the pie, so you can be quite certain that it will set when you pour it into the finished pie – it would be a disaster if when you cut into your precious pie, a torrent of unset 'jelly' greeted your knife!

To make the jelly, first chop the onions coarsely and put them into a large saucepan. Pour on the water and add the pepper and the chopped herbs. You should now drop in any bits of skin or gristle trimmed from the meat, together with a few pork bones from the butcher. If possible, add a 15cm (6″) square of skin cut from some belly pork as this is rich in the gelatinous substances required to make the jelly set. Now bring the stock to the boil, then cover and simmer *gently* for about two hours. Check the pan occasionally and replenish the lost water as necessary – use boiling water to do this so as not to take the stock off the boil.

When the two hours are up, strain the stock into another pan and boil briskly until reduced by half, then cover and leave to cool. When the stock is completely cold, lift off any fat that has come to the surface. If you are lucky, the stock may well have set; if not, don't worry, you can use some bought gelatine – just follow the instructions on the packet. If you *do* have to resort to bought gelatine, the jelly will be a little tougher than it otherwise would be, but still perfectly satisfactory.

Preparing the filling
Cut up the trimmed meat into ½cm (¼″) dice using a sharp knife. I find the quickest way to do this is first to cut the meat into ½cm slabs, then, taking one slab at a time, cut it into ½cm strips, and finally cut these the other way to produce the ½cm dice. Put the diced meat into a bowl, add the other ingredients and mix all together thoroughly.

Making the crust
Put the flour into a bowl, add the salt and stir well. In a small pan, heat the milk and fats together until all the fat has melted. Make a well in the flour and pour the fat and milk mixture into it. Stir all the flour into the liquid, and as soon as the pastry is cool enough to handle, knead it for a few minutes to produce a nice stiff paste.

For the next stage you will need something to mould the crust round; traditionally, special turned sycamore wood pie moulds were used for this, but you can use a large glass or earthenware jar about 15cm (6″) in diameter instead. If you use a jar, it is best to line the circumference of it with a sheet of grease-proof paper which should be long enough to wrap round the jar at least one and a half times; the free end must be stuck down firmly or else the paper will unravel when the crust is formed. You will also have to cut out a disc of grease-proof paper of the same diameter as the base of the jar to line the bottom of the crust. The reason for using the paper is to make it easier to withdraw the jar from the finished crust; without it this can be quite tricky.

*To make a Melton Mowbray Pie it is important to chop the meat finely
with a sharp knife, not a mincer. When you've prepared the filling,
form the crust round the outside of a greaseproof paper lined pot or
jar, then pack the filling into it. Finally, seal the lid on using the
prongs of a table fork.*

Liberally flour your working surface, and place about
three quarters of the pastry on it. With your fingers, form
the lump of pastry into a flat disc about 22cm (9″) in
diameter. With the backs of your fingers, gradually flatten
the inner part of the disc until you end up with a flat area
the size of the base of your jar and about 1cm (½″) thick;
this will be the base of the pie.

Having formed the base, sprinkle a little flour into it and
then insert the disc of grease-proof paper you made earlier.
Sprinkle a little more flour on top of the paper, and then
stand the lined jar on it. To form the side of the crust, slowly
and evenly work the remaining pastry up the sides of the jar
using your fingers to squeeze the pastry gently upwards. If
you find the pastry slumps down, then it is still too hot and
should be allowed to rest until it firms up a little. Don't
leave it too long, though, or the pastry will become too hard
and may crack when you work it.

Continue working the pastry up the sides of the jar until
the wall of the crust is of a uniform thickness of about 1cm
(⅜″); at this stage the crust should stand about 12.5cm (5″)
high. Leave the crust to harden slightly, and when fairly

solid, withdraw the jar. Do this very slowly and carefully so as to avoid breaking the crust. With a little luck the jar will slide out quite easily, leaving the paper, which can then be carefully peeled away. Finally, remember to remove the piece of paper in the bottom of the crust. Run a thin-bladed knife under the bottom of the crust to part it from the working surface, then leave the crust until it becomes quite hard before assembling the pie.

What can go wrong
If at any time during the making of the crust disaster strikes and it all comes apart or breaks in your hands, don't panic – simply knead the pastry into a lump and start again from the beginning. The beauty of this type of pastry is that you cannot possibly do it any harm, no matter how much it is worked and re-kneaded, unlike for instance, ordinary short crust pastry. If you *do* need to start again – and it's certainly no disgrace if you do, as standing crusts can be a little tricky to make until you get the knack – you may need to warm the pastry in a cool oven, 107°C (225°F), gas mark ¼, until it becomes pliable again. If many cracks appear in the pastry as you work it, then it is too cold, and should be warmed slightly.

Assembling the pie
When the crust has become hard and sturdy, fill it with the prepared filling, pressing it down well so as not to leave any cavities; but do take *great care* that you don't press too hard and burst the crust.

Once the pie is full, trim the side of the crust level with the filling using sharp kitchen scissors – a knife is not nearly so good for this job as it will tend to tear the crust no matter how sharp it is.

Fitting the lid
Roll out the remaining quarter of the pastry about ½cm (¼″) thick to make the lid. Brush the top edges of the pie crust with beaten egg, and with the aid of the rolling pin, lift the lid onto the top of the pie. Using a finger, firm the edge of the lid down gently all the way round and trim off the overhanging excess pastry, using downward strokes of a sharp knife. With the prongs of a table fork press all round the edge of the lid to seal it securely to the standing crust, thereby making a decorative pattern at the same time. With

the point of a knife, make a hole in the centre of the pie and then put a twist of grease-proof paper in it to keep it open, so that steam can escape while the pie is cooking. Cut four decorative leaves out of the pastry trimmings and stick these to the top of the pie with beaten egg. Finally, glaze the whole top of the pie with more beaten egg. The pie is now ready to be baked.

Baking the pie

You can bake the pie as it is, but it's a good idea to give it a little support to prevent the sides bulging and the pie falling apart in the oven. To support the pie, cut a strip of aluminium foil twice as wide as the pie is high, and long enough to wrap round the pie at least twice. Fold the foil lengthwise and grease one side of it; then wrap round the pie tightly with the greased side innermost. Tie it in place with three lengths of string, one tied round 2.5cm (1″) from the top, one round the middle and the remaining length tied 2.5cm (1″) from the bottom. The strings must *not* be tied tightly or else an impression will be left in the pie.

Transfer the pie very carefully to a well-floured baking sheet and bake for half an hour in the middle of an oven preheated to 190°C (375°F), gas mark 5. At the end of this time, turn the oven down to 150°C (300°F), gas mark 2 and reglaze the top of the pie with more beaten egg. Bake for a further two hours, then remove the foil from around the pie and glaze the top and sides with the remaining beaten egg. If when you remove the foil collar the pie looks at all as if it might collapse, replace the foil immediately and only glaze the top. Return to the oven and bake for a further fifteen minutes until the pie is a nice golden brown, then take it out of the oven and leave to cool. When the pie is sufficiently cool and firm, remove the foil collar. Don't attempt to lift the pie off the baking sheet until it is completely cold; slipping a knife with a thin blade under the pie first will make this easier.

When you are sure the pie is completely cold, heat the jellified stock until it just liquifies, then, using a small funnel or jug, pour it into the pie through the hole in the lid. You may need several goes to completely fill it as the stock will take a while to work its way through the pie. The pie should now be stored in a cool place (*not* the fridge) overnight, to allow the jelly to set and the flavour to develop, before it is eaten.

Game pie

This pie, which I make every Christmas, is undoubtedly my favourite hand-raised pie; its flavour is beyond description.

Pastry crust

900g (2lb) wholemeal flour
400g (14oz) butter
55g (2oz) suet
300ml (½pt) milk
½ teaspoon salt
1 beaten egg for glazing

Jelly

pheasant carcasses – see method below
a small handful of fresh parsley and thyme*
3 small carrots coarsely chopped
1 large leek coarsely chopped
1 large potato coarsely chopped
1.2 litres (2pt) water
gelatine – see method below

*If you can't get fresh herbs, use a couple of tablespoons of dried.

Meat filling

2 well-hung pheasants (you could use chicken or other poultry
meat instead if you prefer)
2 hard boiled eggs
340g (12oz) rump steak
2 glasses of port
2 heaped teaspoons ground mace

Forcemeat balls

110g (4oz) wholemeal breadcrumbs
1 teaspoon finely grated onion
110g (4oz) coarsely chopped mushrooms
170g (6oz) butter melted and then cooled
2 eggs
2 teaspoons each of fresh parsley and thyme*
freshly ground black pepper
pinch of salt

*Use the same amount of dried if you haven't got any fresh herbs.

Roast the pheasants for 20 minutes at 190°C (375°F), gas mark 5, and then remove all the meat from them. Boil the carcasses for two hours in a covered pan with all the other ingredients for the jelly except the gelatine. Strain off the stock and reduce by half, then leave to go cold.

Make the forcemeat balls by combining all the ingredients and then, using your hands, form the mixture into balls about the size of golf balls. Cut the steak and pheasant meat into small pieces, keeping the meats separate. Quarter the hard boiled eggs. Finally, make a standing crust exactly as described in the recipe for the Melton Mowbray pie (see page 92).

Assembling the pie

Layer the steak evenly in the bottom of the crust, and on top of this put a thick layer of pheasant meat. On top of the pheasant meat, arrange the quartered eggs and about a third of the forcemeat balls. Sprinkle on half the mace. Follow this with another layer of pheasant and then the remaining forcemeat balls. Finish filling the pie with the remaining pheasant meat and sprinkle on the remaining mace.

Now trim the top of the pie with scissors and install a lid on top as for the Melton Mowbray pie. The lid can be decorated with leaves cut from the pastry scraps. Through the hole in the centre of the lid pour in the port and 2 tablespoons of stock. Glaze the top of the pie with beaten egg and wrap a foil collar round the sides. Bake the pie in a preheated oven at 180°C (350°F), gas mark 4 for 35 minutes, then turn the oven down to 150°C (300°F), gas mark 2, reglaze and bake for a further 2¼ hours. Reglaze the top again and also glaze the sides if the pie looks strong enough to stand up without the foil; then return the pie to the oven for a further fifteen minutes to brown. When cooked, remove from the oven and allow to cool undisturbed, taking the foil band off as soon as the crust is firm enough to stand without support.

When the pie is nearly cold, dissolve the gelatine in the remaining stock (see gelatine packet for amount to use) and pour into the pie. The pie will be ready to cut the following day, but is better for keeping a little longer. Don't keep the pie in the fridge or the flavour won't develop properly.

PATÉS AND TERRINES

There is much confusion about the terms paté and terrine; while everyone knows what a paté is, many people are a little unsure about what exactly constitutes a terrine, and so a little explanation is in order. Of course, both the terms paté and terrine are French – like so many kitchen and culinary terms. Paté translated simply means 'paste', and invariably refers to one made of highly seasoned meat or liver. The definition of terrine, on the other hand, is slightly more complicated: literally translated it means 'earthenware pot', but the French use the term to describe not a smooth sort of paté (that is, meat paste) but one that contains chunks of meat or other goodies arranged either in layers inside the paté, or else distributed evenly throughout it. (Incidentally, lest the French should get all the credit for the creation of these delicious dishes, I should point out that in Britain potted meats – which are virtually identical to paté – have been made for centuries.)

Commercially, patés are another potential dustbin for the meat industry to put all its low quality meat and other non–meat animal scraps into. Even though patés do fare better than meat pies in that they have to have a minimum 'meat' content of 70 per cent, only half of this has to be lean meat; the other half can be fat, gristle or any of the other rubbish mentioned in chapter 3.

Homemade patés and terrines

To make your own patés and terrines you will need a good quality mincer, as you will have to mince the ingredients very finely. The sort used for making sausages and burgers (see Chapter 3) is ideal. Only mincers with a proper rotating knife type cutting arrangement are suitable; ordinary ones that use a rotating plate are not suitable. Make sure you have a fairly fine plate for your mincer as you will need this to get the paté or terrine to the right consistency.

Other than a good mincer, the only items you may have to buy specially are dishes to cook your patés and terrines in. I always think that glazed earthenware pots, either round or rectangular, look the nicest, and since you will usually want to serve your patés in the pots they were made in, looks are an important consideration. Also available are rectangular enamelled cast iron pots; these are excellent, because cast iron spreads the heat very evenly during cooking.

Unfortunately they are also very pricey, so on balance I prefer to stick with earthenware. Whatever type of dish you choose, it should ideally be about 5–10cm (2–4″) deep, and if possible have a lid, although this isn't essential. You will also need a shallow tray to stand the pots of paté in while they are being cooked. This should be deep enough to take enough water to come half way up the sides of the pots; a meat roasting tin is ideal for this purpose.

Meat for patés and terrines

As a general rule, the best patés and terrines are made from roughly equal amounts of lean meat, fatty meat and something strongly flavoured like liver or well-hung game. Even so, there is room for experimentation, and this rule, like so many rules, can often be broken to good advantage. For instance, a very robust paté can be made using various sorts of livers as the only 'meat' ingredient. In fact, for the very smoothest patés it is usually desirable to use very little or no actual meat, as this can be too fibrous; for these specially smooth patés, liver is the natural choice.

Any type or cut of meat can be used, although pork is most often used because of its relatively bland flavour and its inherent fattiness, both of which enable it to act as a culinary backdrop to more robustly flavoured ingredients. Because the meat will be very finely minced, you can use cheap cuts for the bulk of the meat, although using a proportion of better, more tender cuts adds a definite smoothness to the more special patés. Whatever meats you choose, remember that if all the meat you use is very lean, the paté will tend to be dry and unappetizing. To avoid this, always use an equal quantity of a really fatty cut like belly pork with very lean meat, or alternatively you can mince some pork-back fat with the meat. This is especially important with super-lean game meats.

Choice of seasonings

Since patés and terrines are eaten cold, they do need to be well seasoned; cold food always tastes far more bland than it would it if were hot. For this reason, be especially generous with the herbs and spices, and this is doubly important since spices and herbs also act as natural preservatives. Good spices to use are mace, nutmeg, cloves, cinnamon, cardamom, ginger, cumin, coriander, allspice, fenugreek and the various peppers. If you use herbs, try to choose nice aromatic ones like rosemary, thyme, sage and basil, as these flavour the meats far more effectively than the less aromatic sorts. As always, try if at all possible to use only fresh herbs, and the best way to ensure that you always have plenty of fresh herbs on hand is to grow your own (see Chapter 11).

To extend the meat in your patés you can add some fresh wholemeal breadcrumbs or even rolled oats, but don't use much more than about 90g (3oz) in every pound of paté mixture unless it includes a large proportion of strongly flavoured ingredients such as lambs' or pigs' liver. Soak the breadcrumbs or oats in a little milk or wine before using them.

Finally, wines or spirits such as sherry, port and brandy can be included in more special recipes to add a mellow richness; cream too can be added to good effect. You should remember, though, that while wines and spirits tend to act as preservatives, enabling patés to be kept longer, cream has the opposite effect, and so is best reserved for patés that are going to be eaten fairly quickly. Another way to add creaminess without affecting the keeping qualities is to use butter instead of cream.

Clarified butter

Once you have cooked your paté you will need to seal it with clarified butter. Clarified butter is made by melting ordinary butter in a saucepan and then continuing to heat it carefully until the vigorous bubbling has subsided – the bubbling is due to the small amount of water in the butter being boiled off. Be very careful not to brown the butter, so keep the heat gentle. Strain the hot butter through a piece of fine muslin folded in half. All the water and other impurities which would encourage the butter to go rancid have now been removed, and what is left is virtually pure butter fat, an ideal seal for patés.

BASIC METHODS

Basic paté recipe

All patés are made in roughly the same way, and this recipe for an excellent everyday paté illustrates the general method. For the quantities given below you will need a pot with a capacity of about 750ml (1¼pt) to cook the paté in, or else several smaller ones.

225g (½lb) lean pork – hand, leg or shoulder*
225g (½lb) belly pork
225g (½lb) pigs' liver
1 small onion
1 tablespoon butter
2 teaspoons ground mace
½ teaspoon grated nutmeg
1 clove of garlic, finely chopped
¼ teaspoon ground ginger
2 tablespoons chopped fresh sage – use dried if fresh not
   available

*Remove any gristle, bone and skin first before weighing the
meat. The herbs should be fresh and the spices freshly
ground if at all possible (except for the ginger, which is too
hard to grind yourself). If you can't get fresh herbs, use
about the same amount of dried instead.

Mince the meats and liver as finely as possible, using the
finest plate of your mincer; mincing meat is far easier if you
cut it into strips first and feed them into the mincer one at a
time. Chop the onion finely, fry until golden brown in the
butter, then mince. Combine the minced meats, liver and
onion in a bowl. Add the garlic, the spices and sage, and
then mix everything together well. Now put the whole lot
through the mincer twice using the fine plate. Having
minced the paté, grease your paté pot(s) well with butter and
then spoon the paté mixture into them. Lay a piece of well
greased grease-proof paper across the tops of the pots, and if
your pots have lids, put them on; if they haven't, just cover
the tops with a piece of foil.
    Stand the pots in a shallow tray, and fill the tray with
enough hot water to come half-way up the sides of the pots.
Then place the tray in the middle of an oven preheated to
160°C (325°F), gas mark 3. Cooking the paté in a tray of
water, or au bain marie as they say in France, ensures that
it cooks evenly, without burning; if you are using cast iron
pots the water bath should be unnecessary.
    The paté should be cooked for between 1½ and 2 hours,
depending on the size of the pots – if you pack it into one
large pot it will take longer than if you use several smaller
ones. To check that the paté is cooked, lift the lid or foil
covering and grease-proof paper; if it is firm and has shrunk
away from the sides of the pot, it's cooked – if not, leave it a

little longer. When it is cooked, take the tray out of the oven, lift out the pots, and then leave to cool with the lids or foil in place.

Sealing the paté
When the paté has been cooling for an hour or so, pour off any juices that have come out during the cooking and seal the paté by pouring on melted clarified butter, covering the top of the paté by about ½cm (¼"). Leave to cool and set solid overnight. You should, if possible, keep your paté in a cool place for two or three days before eating it, to allow the flavour to develop.

Once sealed in clarified butter, the paté will keep in the fridge for at least a week to ten days, or can even be put in the deep freeze, where it will keep for several months. Personally, I think freezing paté spoils its flavour, so I always avoid doing this if I can. A better way of making your paté keep, is to press it – using either one of those little presses you can buy specially for the job (if your local kitchen shop doesn't stock them, see page 159 for the name and address of a supplier), or else with a circle of hard wood cut to suit your pot and weighed down with a large stone or similar object. Before pressing, always allow the paté to cool and set slightly. Press the paté overnight, and the following day, remove the press and seal the paté with clarified butter as before. Pressing paté expresses any excess juice and ensures there are no air pockets – both of which encourage the growth of bacteria and similar nasties that would make your paté go off. As an added bonus, pressed patés have a much firmer and closer texture. Pressed paté should keep for several months in the fridge, provided the butter seal remains intact and the pots are kept covered with their lids or with aluminium foil.

Serving paté
I usually serve my patés in the pots they were made in, but you can, if you prefer, turn them out of their pots onto a plate. If you decide you would like to serve them like this, it is a good idea to line the greased pots with thin strips of derinded streaky bacon or 'lard leaves' made by cutting pork back fat into thin slices and then beating the slices wafer thin with a wooden mallet. You can then cut the fat into decorative leaf shapes with a sharp knife. Lining the pots in this way not only makes the paté or terrine look more

attractive on the table, it also helps it to stay in one piece when you come to turn it out onto a plate.

Turning out

To turn a paté out of its pot, run the blade of a small knife round the edges of the paté and then place a plate over the top. Carefully invert the dish and give it a sharp downward jerk; the paté should fall neatly onto the plate. If it doesn't, stand the pot in a pan of boiling water for a few seconds and try again.

Making terrines

Terrines can be made by adapting any paté recipe. They make an eye-catching centrepiece for a buffet meal if turned out onto a plate or board. To make a terrine, you should choose a favourite paté recipe, but instead of mincing all the meat, save a proportion of the best of it and cut it into strips or chunks. In French culinary jargon this chopped meat is called the *salpicon*. To assemble the terrine, grease and line your pot with lard leaves or streaky bacon strips, then half fill it with the finely minced mixture. Now arrange the strips or chunks of meat on top of the paste and cover with the remaining mixture. The terrine can now be cooked exactly as you would a paté, then, if required, pressed. If you like, you can put more than one salpicon layer in the terrine or even have no layers at all, simply mixing the salpicon into the paste instead. Other tasty morsels, like seedless raisins soaked in brandy, or nuts, can be added to the salpicon to make the terrine even more special.

MORE RECIPES

To cook each of the patés below you will need a pot or pots with a total capacity of about 750ml (1¼pt). As always, the herbs should if possible be fresh, and the spices freshly ground, except for the ginger, which should be bought ready-ground.

Liver paté

225g (½lb) lambs' liver
225g (½lb) pigs' liver
170g (6oz) wholemeal breadcrumbs, soaked in a little milk or wine

1 small onion
56ml (2fl oz) cream
1 tablespoon butter
1 tablespoon brandy (optional)
1 finely chopped clove of garlic
2 teaspoons ground mace
½ teaspoon ground cloves
1 tablespoon chopped fresh (or dried) thyme
¼ teaspoon ground ginger
½ teaspoon grated nutmeg
¼ teaspoon ground black pepper
3 bay leaves

Chop the onion finely and fry in the butter until golden brown. Mince the livers and fried onion finely and then combine with the remaining ingredients, except the bay leaves, in a large bowl, mixing very thoroughly. Pass the mixture through the fine plate of the mincer twice, then fill your well-greased pot(s) and arrange the bay leaves on top. Cook *au bain marie* (see page 101) in an oven preheated to 160°C (325°F), gas mark 3, for about one and a half hours. Finish off in the same way as for the basic paté (see page 102).

Beef paté

340g (¾lb) rump steak – include any fat
110g (¼lb) lambs' liver
225g (½lb) belly pork
1 small onion
1 tablespoon butter
56ml (2fl oz) port or other red wine (optional)
½ teaspoon ground cloves
2 cloves of garlic, finely chopped
1 rounded teaspoon ground mace
1½ teaspoons ground allspice
½ teaspoon ground black pepper
1 tablespoon each of chopped fresh (or dried) rosemary, sage
   and thyme

Chop the onion finely and fry in the butter until just browning. Mince the steak, pork, liver and fried onion as finely as possible. Combine the minced ingredients with the spice, herbs and wine, then pass the mixture twice through the fine plate of the mincer. Pot and cook *au bain marie* (see page 101) for about one and a half hours (or until cooked) in an oven preheated to 160°C (325°F), gas mark 3. Finish in the usual way (see page 102).

Pheasant or chicken terrine

You will need a pot with a capacity of at least 1.2 litres (2pt) for this recipe.

2 dressed pheasants or one chicken
340g (12oz) belly pork
110g (4oz) wholemeal breadcrumbs, soaked in milk or wine
1 small onion
1 tablespoon butter
56ml (2fl oz) brandy or orange juice
strips of derinded streaky bacon to line dish
4 cloves of garlic, finely chopped
4 tablespoons finely chopped fresh (or dried) parsley
1 teaspoon ground mace
½ teaspoon ground black pepper

Roast the pheasants or chicken in the oven for half the time needed to completely cook the meat. Now remove all the meat you can from the carcass, being careful to pull at least some of it off in big pieces. Put about 340g (12oz) of the large pieces of meat on one side, and mince the remainder as finely as possible. Similarly, mince the belly pork and then put the minced meats into a large bowl, together with the breadcrumbs and the herbs and spices. Next, chop the onion finely, fry in the butter until transparent, mince finely and add to the other ingredients in the bowl. Pour on the brandy or orange juice, mix everything together thoroughly to form a paste, then pass it all through the fine plate of the mincer twice.

Blanch the strips of bacon in a pan of boiling water for one minute to draw out some of the bacon flavour, and then use them to line a well greased dish. Half fill the dish with the paste, then chop up the meat you set on one side into strips or cubes and arrange this on top of the paste. Cover with the remaining paste mixture and then cover and cook *au bain marie* (see page 101) in an oven preheated to 160°C (325°F), gas mark 3, as you would for paté. When cooked, allow to cool slightly and then if possible, press and leave overnight to go completely cold. In the morning, cover with clarified butter and store until required. To serve, turn out onto a plate or board.

8.
BREWING
BEER

At one time, the brewing of beer was very much a domestic affair, and just about every household that could afford to do so brewed its own. Nowadays, although home brewing has undergone something of a renaissance in recent years, most of our beer is brewed in large automated breweries equipped with hardware that would look more at home in a chemical factory or oil refinery than a brewery.

Many of us who look fastidiously at the ingredients of the cans and packets of the food we buy, never give a thought to what might be in the beer we drink at the pub. Not that if we did think about it we would be any the wiser, as alcoholic drinks that contain more than 1.2 per cent alcohol don't have to carry a list of ingredients! Even the weak, imitation 'lagers' that have become so popular through hugely expensive image-selling advertising campaigns are stronger than that. In West Germany, things are very different. There it is illegal to brew beer with anything other than water, yeast, hops and malt. This law, called *das Rheinheitsgebot*, was introduced by King Wilhelm IV way back in 1516 and remains in force to this day. Even so, attempts are being made by other brewers within the EEC to have the *Reinheitsgebot* rescinded, since their beers do not come up to its laudably stringent standards, and until recently were denied access to the German market. British beers in particular have been criticized on the grounds that the various additives used to tart them up represent a serious health hazard. The German brewers have claimed that formaldehyde is used in British beer, a claim which the British Brewers' Society has hotly rejected on the grounds that this would be illegal even by British laws. However, what the British brewers *do* use, is a chemical called dimethylpolysiloxane, which acts as a foam control agent during fermentation. This enables the brewers to cram more beer into their fermenting vessels by reducing the size of the yeast head that would naturally sit atop the vats of fermenting beer. Not only is dimethylpolysiloxane a suspected carcinogen in itself, but it can also contain formaldehyde as a contaminant, and this also is carcinogenic. It would seem that the Germans may be right after all.

Other additives which find their way into your pint include caramel, a colouring which has long been under suspicion of being toxic, and has been found to produce blood disorders in test animals. Of all the food colourings, ammonium caramel – the sort brewers use – is the one most likely to be consumed in amounts which exceed the so called 'safe' daily dose; even the British government's own Food Additives and Contaminants Committee recognized this as far back as 1979. Nonetheless, nothing has been done, and huge amounts of this dangerous and unnecessary colouring are still added to our food, and, of course, our beer.

Yet more additives that have never really been proved safe go into your pint; alginate esters for example, are used to produce a head on the beer when it is served, an effect that could be achieved naturally if the brewers used more malt in their beers instead of cheap substitutes. Gum acacia is another 'heading' agent commonly used, and has been linked with various forms of hypersensitivity; even the somewhat conservative World Health Organization has called for more research into its safety. Even at the very early stage of beer making when barley is turned into malt, chemical additives are used to speed things up to the advantage of the industry, not the consumer. One of the chemicals used is potassium bromate (a sort of bleach) which has been found to cause various bowel and stomach disorders.

Over the last sixty or seventy years, the strength of pub beer has declined markedly. In fact, an old brewing text book sums this up rather revealingly by saying 'It is an interesting commentary on the weak and non-resisting low gravity beverages of today that not very long ago farmers used to brew their own beers on farm premises under conditions which today would be definitely impossible.' (That book was written more than thirty years ago!). Nowadays beers are so weak that brewers consider it more or less essential to add sulphur dioxide in one form or another to their draught beers to act as a preservative. True, sulphur dioxide has been used in wine since Roman times, but it is nonetheless a dangerous additive that has been responsible for several deaths and is particularly hazardous to asthmatics.

Hand in hand with the reduction in strength has gone the reduction in the quantity of malt used. This has had serious ramifications, since malt is the main ingredient of beer, apart from water, and is the one upon which its whole character and flavour crucially depends. Worse still, a proportion of the malt can be replaced by sugar, cereal flours or even potato starch, all of which are cheaper to use than malt. These 'adjuncts', as they are known, although giving the beer alcoholic strength, add little in the way of flavour and character to the traditional pint, and so consequently pub beer lacks body and tastes thin. It's much the same story with hops; nowadays the only thing considered to be important is their bittering quality; gone are considerations of flavour and aroma, once prized above all else. Consequently, the old long-cherished varieties like Goldings and Fuggles have largely given way to new, more bitter varieties bred only for bitterness and not for flavour. As you would expect, using these more bitter hops is a great money-saver for the brewer, since far fewer hops now need to be used to produce a beer of a given bitterness than with the older varieties.

HOW BEER IS MADE

The ingredient which provides most (if not all) of the strength, and much of the flavour and character of beer, is malt. Malt starts life as barley, but it has to be processed to convert the starch in the grain which the yeast cannot ferment into alcohol, into malt sugars which it can. The first part of this process is called *malting*, and involves wetting the barley grains and allowing them to germinate. During germination, natural enzymes are produced which break down the large starch molecules in the grain into smaller starch molecules and malt sugars. If the process were allowed to continue unchecked, the developing barley plant would use up all this newly produced food, and there would be none left for the yeast to ferment. To prevent this calamity, the little barley plants are killed off by heating the grain in a kiln. If after the malt is completely dry the kilning process is continued, the malt gradually darkens to produce the so-called 'coloured' malts, which are used in small amounts to add extra colour and flavour to the beer. Amongst the most useful of these malts is the beautiful amber coloured crystal malt which is often used to add a pleasant, nutty flavour to bitter. The really well-roasted malts like chocolate and black malt are used to add colour and roundness to the darker milds and brown ales.

Mashing

The next stage of the conversion of starch into fermentable sugars is called mashing. This involves mixing the malt to a porridge-like consistency with hot water and keeping it warm for several hours. During mashing, the enzymes which were produced when the barley grains germinated during malting, break down the starch further to form fermentable malt sugars. These malt sugars are basically of two types: maltose and the various dextrins. Maltose ferments very rapidly, whereas the dextrins ferment much more slowly, and so help to prevent the beer from going flat while in storage.

When all the starch has been converted to sugars, the dissolved malt sugars are drained off the malt in the form of dark, sticky liquid known as 'sweet wort' (pronounced wert). The sugars still held by the malt grains are then washed out with hot water in a process called *sparging*.

Next, the sweet wort is boiled with hops in a boiler known as a copper, in memory of the metal they were once made of. At this stage, extra sugar can be added to give the beer more strength. Boiling serves several important functions: it sterilizes the wort so that no harmful organisms survive to spoil the beer; it evaporates excess water, and so concentrates the wort; and last but not least, it effectively extracts the flavour and bitterness from the hops and helps to ensure that the beer will end up bright and clear. The latter occurs because tannins in the hops precipitate the malt proteins, which if not removed would make the beer permanently cloudy. After boiling, the hopped wort is cooled, yeast is added, and the beer is allowed to ferment.

Fermentation

Once the first vigorous fermentation is over, the 'green' beer, as it is now known, is siphoned off the sediment into casks, where a much slower secondary fermentation of the dextrinous malt sugars gives the beer a slight fizz or condition. After a few weeks of maturing in a cool place, the beer is ready to drink.

BREWING AT HOME

Using Kits
Having read about how beer is brewed traditionally, you could be forgiven for thinking home brewing sounds like a lot of trouble. Don't worry – there are lots of short-cuts you can use. For a start, you won't be malting your own barley, as this would need a lot of room and special equipment. Malting aside, by far the most time-consuming part of brewing, and the part with the most pitfalls for the beginner, is mashing. Fortunately, if you don't feel inclined to do your own mashing, this can be dispensed with also. Instead, you can buy your wort ready made from the homebrew shop in a concentrated form known as malt extract. You don't even have to do any boiling if you don't want to, as you can buy malt extract already flavoured with hops. These cans of hopped malt extract are known more commonly as beer kits, which is a pretty good description, since all you need to do is dissolve the contents in water and add sugar and yeast. There are other forms of beer kit based on dry ingredients, but these are nowhere near as good as the sort that comes in a can.

Using one of the many malt-extract-based beer kits on the market is the quickest way of brewing beer at home, but somehow, beer made from these kits always tastes inferior to that made by the other slightly more elaborate methods. However, one easy way of improving matters is to use two kits for each brew instead of just one; for example, if the standard directions on the can say use 1kg (2¼lb) of sugar plus the contents of the can for a five gallon (22.5 litre) brew, use *two* cans and 1kg of sugar to make the same amount of beer. Another easy improvement can be effected by using genuine brewer's yeast (see page 112). One unavoidable drawback of beer kits, however, is that many of them contain additives – notably caramel.

Equipment for homebrewing

To brew beer from kits you will need little more than a large
fermenting bin and a length of rubber or plastic tubing to
siphon the beer into your final storage vessels. What sort of
vessel(s) you choose is up to you. Some people use bottles,
but I find this tiresome and fiddly. It's far more convenient
to use a single large container and have your beer on
draught. The most common bulk vessel is a pressure barrel,
and there are many different sorts available. These are ideal
if you like your beer very gassy, but you will need to buy a
carbon dioxide cylinder and the associated paraphernalia to
go with it in order to keep the barrel pressurized. A better,
and far cheaper solution is to use one of the large polythene
cubes known as polypins which off-licences sell cheap
draught wines from; when empty, most shops will let you
have one very cheaply.

To brew beer using malt extract, you will additionally
need a kitchen sieve, a 1 litre (2pt) heat-proof jug and a pan
of about 10 litres (18pt) capacity (full to the brim) to boil the
beer in; an aluminium or stainless steel preserving pan is
ideal. If you can afford one, a large electric boiler is very
handy for boiling up all the brewing water beiore use (see
recipe for Malt Extract Beer, on page 112). A large stainless
steel wash boiler is ideal. If you have one of these you can
boil all of your beer, not just a small part of it, and this
definitely improves the quality of the beer. A thermometer is
also a handy addition to your brewing kit, as it takes the
guess-work out of measuring temperatures.

Whatever method you use to brew your beer, it is vitally
important that all the equipment used is thoroughly clean.
The best way to clean it is with hot soapy water, but rinse
everything very thoroughly to remove every trace of soap or
else it may taint your beer. Soap will also destroy the head
on your pint – if you care about such things.

Brewing from malt exract

The next step up from using kits is to use unhopped malt
extract and add your own hops, and perhaps other
ingredients as well. Because you are hopping the beer
yourself, you will need to do *some* boiling, but you need only
boil 10 litres or so of the beer, and it can be done in a large
pan on top of the stove.

RECIPES

Malt extract beer

1.8kg (4lb) malt extract (Edme DMS is the best)
85–110g (3–4oz) of Goldings hops (depending on how bitter
  you like your beer)
900g (2lb) white sugar
yeast – see below
27 litres (6 gallons) of water

If possible, boil the water and allow it to cool before using it
to brew your beer. When cool, leave it for a couple of days
for the (now) insoluble hardness salts to settle out of the
water, then siphon the softened water off into another
container, leaving the last few inches behind. This treatment
will remove any temporary hardness and drive off chlorine
(put in by the Water Board), both of which will be injurious
to the flavour. If you can't be bothered to boil the water,
don't worry, it's not essential.

Put about 5.7 litres (10pt) of water into your pan and
bring to the boil. When boiling, remove from the heat and
empty into it the malt extract and sugar, remembering to
rinse out the last of the malt extract from the tins with a
little hot water taken from the pan. Stir well to dissolve the
malt extract and sugar, then sprinkle in the hops and return
the pan to the heat.

As the wort (see page 109) nears boiling point, be sure to
stir it continuously or you will have hops and froth spilling
over the side of the pan. Boil briskly for 45 minutes, then
take the pan off the heat and allow it to stand for five
minutes. Now bail the wort out of the pan with a jug and
pour it through a kitchen sieve into your fermenting bin.
The hops will have absorbed a considerable amount of the
valuable wort, so before discarding, rinse them with a little
water and strain this into the bin as well.

Top up to about 25 litres (5½ gallons) with cold water and,
after making sure the liquid isn't hotter than about 24°C
(75°F), add the yeast.

Yeast
The easiest sort of yeast to use is the dried brewing yeast
available in little sachets from home brew shops. The trouble
with this type of yeast is that it isn't the kind professional
brewers use, and can spoil the flavour of your beer.

After boiling the wort with the hops, strain it into your fermenting bin, top up with cold water and add the yeast. Once fermentation is under way, skim off with a slotted spoon any brown scum that appears.

Fortunately, genuine brewer's yeast is now easy to obtain and is sold, usually in liquid culture form, from good home brew shops. Recently, genuine brewer's yeast has become available in dried form. I have used this yeast for quite a number of brews, and it seems very good – it's certainly a delight to use, since you just sprinkle it into the beer as you would ordinary yeast.

If you decide to use a brewer's yeast in liquid form, life isn't quite as easy, since you can't just dump it into the beer as you would dried yeast. Instead, it must be activated first by making a yeast starter (in a rather similar way to making a cheese starter). You will have to remember to make up the starter a couple of days before you intend to brew your beer. To make the starter, put 2 tablespoons of malt extract into a *clean* jug, then add 290ml (½pt) of hot water, stirring well to dissolve the extract. When dissolved, add 150ml (¼pt) of cold water and pour the liquid into a scrupulously clean milk bottle. Check that the bottle of wort feels cool to the touch, then shake up the sachet of brewer's yeast and pour it into the bottle. Seal the bottle with a plug of cotton wool and store in a warm place for a couple of days until you see signs of fermentation, at which point the starter is ready to use.

Don't add the starter to your beer until you are sure it is fermenting and bubbles can be seen rising to the surface.

Once the starter bottle *is* fermenting, you can safely keep it in a cool place (not the fridge) for a couple of days if it's not convenient to brew immediately.

Skimming

Within twenty-four to thirty-six hours of adding the yeast to your beer, you should begin to see a yeast head forming on the surface. Keep a close eye on this. If it looks brown, as it may do in the early stages of fermentation, then skim the brown bits off with a slotted spoon and discard them.

Barreling

After about five days, the initial vigorous fermentation will be over and the frothy yeast head will have disappeared, leaving only the occasional bubble to be seen rising to the surface. At this point, the beer should be siphoned off (or drawn from a tap fitted near the bottom of your fermenting bin) into a pressure barrel or polypin (see page 111), leaving the yeast deposit behind.

Once the beer has finished fermenting, transfer it to a polypin or pressure barrel.

To use a pressure barrel, siphon the beer into it, then add a solution made by dissolving 110g (4oz) of white sugar in 290ml (½pt) of hot water. This priming solution will provide food for the small amount of yeast left in the beer to produce gas to pressurize the barrel and give the beer a fizz. When you start drinking the beer, the pressure in the barrel will drop and you will have to use a cylinder of carbon dioxide to repressurize it.

If you use a polypin you will save yourself the expense of buying carbon dioxide. Siphon your beer into it, then if you like your beer to have a fizz, prime it with sugar as you would a pressure barrel. (Personally I don't like fizzy beer, so I never prime mine.) Now screw the tap on and make sure it is in the open position so as to allow carbon dioxide produced by the secondary fermentation to escape. To seal the beer against dust and insects, push a loose plug of cotton wool into the mouth of the tap. Store the polypin in a cool place – ideally about 15°C (60°F) – for about two weeks or until you are ready to start drinking the beer, then turn the polypin over so that the tap is now in the serving position; do remember to close the tap first! Turning the polypin over will stir up the sediment, so be sure to turn it over at least 24 hours before you want to drink the beer, in order to give the sediment time to settle again.

The beauty of the polypin is that as the beer is drunk it collapses, so preventing air getting into the beer and spoiling it. But if at any time it starts to bulge slightly, as will happen if the gas from the secondary fermentation is being produced faster than you are drinking the beer, then you will just have to draw some beer off and drink it!

Fining
Whether you use a polypin or a pressure barrel, if after a fortnight your beer isn't clear, you will have to use a special clearing preparation called *finings*. The best all round beer finings is 'isinglass', which is prepared from the swim bladder of the Sturgeon fish. The best way to buy it is in liquid form – just follow the directions on the bottle. Isinglass should clear your beer completely in under five days.

Yield: about 22.5 litres (5 gallons).

Mild beer

1.8kg (4lb) malt extract
170g (6oz) crushed black malt
85g (3oz) roasted barley
450g (1lb) Muscavado sugar
450g (1lb) white sugar
55g (2oz) Fuggles hops
yeast – preferably genuine brewer's
27 litres (6 gallons) water

Essentially, the method is identical to that for the Malt Extract Beer recipe (see page 112). If possible, boil and cool the water to drive off chlorine and remove hardness, but this isn't essential. To brew the beer, first boil the malt extract, sugars, black malt, roasted barley and hops for 45 minutes in about 5.7 litrès (10 pt) of water, then strain into the fermenting bin, remembering to rinse the hops. Top up to 25 litres (5½ gallons) with cold water, and add the yeast. From then on, treat exactly as for the bitter.

Yield: about 22.5 litres (5 gallons).

Mashing

The ultimate in customized home brewing is beer brewed from scratch using malt grains which you mash yourself rather than simply buying the end product (malt extract) in cans. Brewing beer in this way gives you complete control over how your beer will look and taste: beer made by mashing is truly your own creation. Mashing is not that difficult, but you do need to pay attention to detail, and you may have to improvize a special mash tub to do it in.

Mashing malt involves mixing it with hot water and keeping it at the correct mashing temperature of around 65–70°C (150–160°F) for several hours to enable the enzymes to do their work. To do this effectively, you will need some form of insulated tub. Traditionally, a wooden cask with one end knocked out often served the purpose. Sadly, nowadays casks are hard to come by and tend to be rather expensive, although reasonably priced second-hand ones do come up for sale occasionally. It is also still possible to buy small, purpose-made wooden mash tubs at a reasonable price (see page 159). Although I do have a wooden mash tub, it is quite large, so I only use it when I am mashing a lot of malt, and being wooden, it needs careful cleaning and looking after. For smaller mashes, such as those needed to make the beers in the following recipes, I use a home-made insulated plastic tub. To make one of these you will need two buckets. The smaller one, which will hold the mash, needs to have a capacity of about 5.7 litres (10pt). The larger one should have a diameter about 10cm (4″) larger than that of the small bucket. To make the mash tub, cut a hole in the lid of the larger bucket to suit the diameter of the small bucket and then push the small bucket into it; when you cut the hole, make sure you don't make it too large – this needs to be a tight fit. The lid is now fitted onto the large bucket

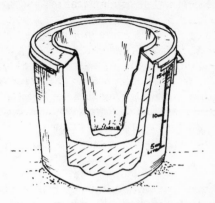

Cross section of the homemade insulated mash tub.

with the space between the two buckets stuffed with glass fibre to act as thermal insulation (see illustration above for further details).

In this little mash tub you can quite easily mash 1.8–2.3kg (4–5lb) of malt, which is an ideal amount to work with if you have never mashed malt before. Unfortunately, this small quantity of malt won't make a particularly strong beer, so you will still have to use some bought malt extract to supplement it. Even so, these 'hybrid' brews do taste far nicer than beer made solely with bought malt extract.

'Hybrid' best bitter

1.8kg (4lb) crushed pale malt
255g (9oz) crystal malt
1.35kg (3lb) malt extract (Edme DMS for preference)
900g (2lb) white sugar
85–110g (3–4oz) Goldings hops
yeast (see below)
31.5 litres (7 gallons) water

If possible, boil and cool the water as described in the first bitter recipe (see page 112); the reason you need rather more this time is because some will be absorbed by the malt. The first part of the brewing process is the mashing of the malt. This should be done in the evening, since it will have to stand overnight. Place the crushed malt and cyrstal malt in your mash tub and mix together well with your fingers. Now bring three pints of water to the boil; you may need this for adjusting the temperature of the mash slightly. In another pan, heat about 5.1 litres (9pt) of the water to 82°C (180°F) using a good quality thermometer to check the temperature. It is important you get this temperature right, since if it is too low, the mash will be too cool for the enzymes to work properly, and if it is too high the enzymes may be destroyed, and once again the mash won't work. When the water has reached the correct temperature, pour 4 litres (7pt) of it onto the malt, and stir very thoroughly to make sure the mash has an even consistency and that there are no patches of dry malt left on the bottom of the tub. Check the temperature of the mash with the thermometer; if it is somewhere between 66–70°C (152–158°F), then all is well. If it is too low, you should add a little of the boiling water, give the mash a good stir and check the temperature again. If it is too hot, add some cold water. When properly mixed, the mash should have the consistency of thin porridge. If if is too thick, you should add more water; if you use some of the water heated to 82°C, the temperature of the mash shouldn't be altered appreciably by this addition.

Once the mash has the right consistency and is at the correct temperature, put the lid on the mash tub and cover with a couple of thick blankets to keep it warm. Leave to stand overnight in a warm, draught-free place.

Starch end point
In the morning, transfer a drop of the mash liquid to a white plate, using the end of the thermometer. Onto this place a single drop of a solution of iodine, made by mixing equal quantities of tincture of iodine (bought from a chemist) and water (keep this solution in a little bottle for testing future brews). If the mash liquid *immediately* turns dark blue, then not all the starch in the malt has been converted to malt sugars. This means you may have to use a little extra malt extract to make up for the consequent slight loss of strength. The beauty of this hybrid recipe is that even if your mash doesn't work as well as you had hoped, all is not lost, since the situation can easily be rectified with a little bought malt extract, and your beer will still have a strong mashed character imparted by the malt. If you were relying solely on mashing for all the beer's strength, the situation would be more serious, since not only would you have wasted a lot of expensive malt, your beer would contain a great deal of starch which could make it permanently cloudy.

Sparging

Having tested your mash, you must now transfer it to a jelly bag suspended over a bucket and let the sweet wort drain off. Meanwhile, bring 4.5 litres (8pt) of water to the boil, and then carefully pour it onto the malt in the jelly bag, using a jug. Do this slowly, so that the water works its way down through the malt, washing the malt sugars out of the grains. Collect about 5.7 litres (10pt) of wort (see page 109).

Boiling the wort

Pour the wort from the bucket into a pan with a capacity of at least 10 litres (18pt), and add the malt extract, sugar and hops. Bring to the boil, stirring well to prevent the malt extract and sugar burning, and the hops erupting over the side of the pan. Continue boiling for 45 minutes. Then, take the pan off the heat and leave to stand for five minutes before bailing out the hopped wort using a jug and pouring it into your fermenting bin through a kitchen strainer to catch the hops. As always, rinse the wort out of the hops with a little water and add this to the bin.

Top up to the 25 litre (5½ gallon) mark, add the yeast (preferably genuine brewer's yeast) and then ferment as before, being careful to remove any brown scum that rises to the surface. After the vigorous primary fermentation is over, syphon the beer into a polypin or pressure barrel and keep for a couple of weeks before sampling. If necessary, the beer can be fined with isinglass (see page 115).

'Hybrid' mild

A mild beer can be made using the same basic recipe as the preceding, but using 55g (2oz) of Fuggles hops instead of Goldings, substituting 225g (8oz) of black malt and 110g (4oz) of roasted barley for the crystal malt, and replacing 450g (1lb) of the white sugar with the same amount of Muscavado sugar.

SPENT HOPS AND MALT

The spent hops and malt left after you have done your brewing are a very good source of organic matter for your garden, so don't just throw them in the dustbin. You can either add them to your compost heap, or else use them as a mulch around your plants.

9.
WINEMAKING

One of the most infuriating things about buying wine from a shop is the fact that as much as half of the cost is simply tax, or what the Customs and Excise prefers to call 'duty'. Admittedly, with better quality wines *proportionately* less of the price goes to pay the duty, since duty is assessed only on the alcoholic strength of the wine not its quality.

Although home winemaking has grown enormously in popularity over the past 20 years, homemade wines do still have a bad reputation with many people, and are often considered distinctly second best to commercially produced wines. This slander really is quite undeserved, as homemade wines can be easily as good as, and very often superior to many shop-bought wines. Apart from saving money, there is another benefit of making your own wines, and that is that you know exactly what has gone into them. By now surely no one can be unaware of the wine scandals which seem to blow up with monotonous regularity every time it is discovered that dangerous chemicals have been used to tart up some brand or other of commercial wine. Often these adulterations only come to light after someone has actually been poisoned by one of these illegal activities; antifreeze being used to sweeten cheap German wine is a recent example.

Just as worrying though, are the additives that can *legally* be put into wine. One of the worst is sulphur dioxide, which is used in several forms as a preservative. Even though the wine industry's apologists point out that sulphur dioxide has been added to wine since Roman times, it is still nonetheless a very dangerous additive and has actually caused deaths; people with asthma and other respiratory disorders are particularly at risk from its noxious effects. Other dubious additives used by the wine trade range from dried blood, which is used to improve the clarity of wine, to cyanide compounds used to remove hazes from wines contaminated by metals and to improve the colour of red wines. What else gets into wine is anyone's guess, since our food regulations don't require alcoholic drinks with a strength in excess of 1.2% alcohol to carry a list of ingredients – even the weakest wines are far stronger than that! All things considered, there is genuine good reason to be concerned about what finds its way into commercial wines – especially the cheaper sorts, and saving money aside, from a purely health point of view it makes sense to make your own.

SULPHITE

There is very little point in making your own wines if you are going to put into them many of the same additives that you are trying to avoid. Sadly, as home winemaking has become ever more scientific – which in itself is a good thing – so has grown the tendency to use more and more chemicals. By far the most common of these chemicals, is sodium metabisulphite or 'sulphite' as it is commonly known by winemakers. I am sure if you were to ask just about any orthodox home winemaker, they would tell you that it is quite impossible to make wine without it. They are wrong. I haven't used it for years and my wines are certainly none the worse for its absence, in fact I believe they are better. Not only is it possible to make wines without sulphite, you should make your wines without it, since this chemical is simply a source of noxious sulphur dioxide. In commercial wines the legal limit for available sulphur dioxide is 200 parts per million, yet one home winemaking book I looked at recently recommends using amounts of sulphite that would create a sulphur dioxide concentration easily in excess of this level. In the hands of the (reputable) commercial winemaker sulphur dioxide is considerably safer than in those of the home winemaker, since commercially the amount of sulphur dioxide in wine is continuously monitored and maintained within definite limits. In sharp contrast, the home winemaker cannot measure how much sulphur dioxide his or her wine contains and so routinely adds sulphite regardless. This can and does lead to dangerously high sulphur dioxide levels, and is a highly dangerous practice. I can remember many occasions when I have drunk homemade wines, including my own in the days when I used to use sulphite, and have been reduced to a coughing wreck as the highly irritant sulphur dioxide in it gripped my lungs. Make no mistake, sulphite is a dangerous and unnecessary additive and should be avoided.

SAFE ADDITIVES

Not all winemaking additives are harmful, one group of additives in particular are essential to most wines if the fermentation chemistry is to proceed properly. These benign additives are the yeast nutrient salts which help 'feed' the yeast. Without additions of these nutrient salts, many wines would be deficient in nitrogen, and this would lead to the production of large amounts of poisonous substances known collectively as fusel oil.

There are other useful additives which are sometimes used to improve the final appearance of the wine by removing tiny haze forming particles which would otherwise make the wine murky. These additives fall into two categories and are known either as enzymes or finings, but more of them later.

MAKING WINE

Whatever type of wine you make, the first step is to extract the flavour and other essential constituents of the raw ingredients. The raw ingredients can range from flowers or leaves, to fruits and vegetables. Generally speaking, the best wines are made from fruits, although superb wines can be made from vegetables, especially roots. Wines made solely from flowers or leaves are, in my experience, usually rather poor, although if used in *conjunction* with fruits, flowers certainly enhance the bouquet of a wine.

There are many ways of extracting the flavour from the raw ingredients, but as a general rule the less heating the ingredients undergo the better. Using only cold extraction methods not only improves the flavour and bouquet of the finished wine, by conserving delicate volatile constituents which would be lost if heat were used, but also increases the chances of the wine clearing without the use of enzymes or finings (see pages 124 and 125). This is because natural pectin destroying enzymes are present in fruits and vegetables and these are easily inactivated by heat.

All the recipes below, except the last one, which isn't really a proper wine anyway, are for fruit-based wines. In my experience the best way of getting the flavour out of fruit is to mash it up in water and then add sugar and yeast and let the fermentation process extract the flavour. This method is known as 'fermenting on the pulp', and is conducted in a closely covered bucket for between 3 and 10 days in a warm place at around 18–21°C (65–70°F). At the end of this time the wine is strained into a special 4.5 litre (1 gallon) winemaking bottle known as a 'demijohn', and if necessary topped up to just below the neck with water. The demijohn is then sealed with an airlock to prevent dirt, air and insects getting into the wine, and then stored in a warm place as before. The fermentation will continue for several weeks or months before eventually slowing down and finally a layer of sediment will start to collect at the bottom of the demijohn. Once a sediment appears, the wine should be siphoned or 'racked' off into another demijohn, taking care not to suck up any sediment. A golden rule in winemaking is never to leave wine standing on a sediment as the wine may be spoiled by off-flavours produced as the sediment decomposes. Always remember, as soon as a sediment appears – rack the wine.

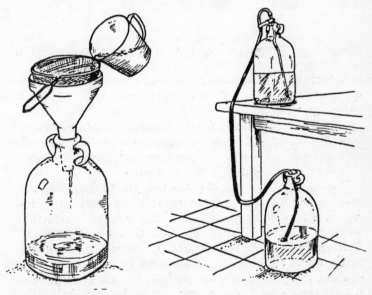

After fermenting on the pulp, strain the wine into a demijohn, and as soon as a substantial sediment appears, rack.

Obviously after the wine has been racked there will be less wine in the new demijohn because of the discarded sediment. In order to prevent too much oxygen getting to the wine and spoiling it, the demijohn should be topped up to the bottom of the neck with a solution made by dissolving 90g (3oz) of white sugar in 290ml (½pt) of warm water. After topping up, the airlock should be replaced and the fermentation will continue, albeit at a very much slower rate. After a while – maybe several months – the fermentation will stop completely and the wine will begin to clear, throwing off another sediment in the process. Once again, rack into another demijohn and top up, but this time with plain tap water. You should now, if possible, move the wine to a cooler place – say between 13–18°C (55–65°F) – and leave it to clear completely, racking whenever a substantial sediment accumulates.

If you are in a hurry and can't wait for the wine to clear naturally, which can sometimes take up to 6 months or more, or if after this length of time it still isn't clear, you will have to resort to some form of remedial measure in the form of enzymes or finings.

Enzymes
One of the most common causes of persistently cloudy wines is a substance called pectin which is found in particularly large amounts in fruits like blackcurrants and gooseberries, and in smaller amounts in vegetables. It isn't pectin in itself that makes a wine cloudy, it is the stabilizing effect it has on haze-producing particles in the wine. Under the action of pectin these microscopic particles cannot fall to the bottom of the demijohn, and so the wine remains stubbornly hazy. To remove the pectin a special pectin destroying enzyme must be used. Enzymes are special proteins which have the ability to perform very specific tasks, which in the case of pectin destroying enzyme is the elimination of pectin. The enzyme is available as a powder or liquid and there are various brands to choose from. I prefer to use liquid versions such as pectolase. The powder sorts often leave difficult to remove particles floating in the wine.

Before using the pectin enzyme you should first check to make sure that there really is pectin in the wine. Do this by putting a teaspoonful of the wine into a small glass and adding three teaspoonfuls of methylated spirit. Now shake the glass to mix the wine with the meths, then leave it to stand for a few minutes. If strings or clots of a jelly-like substance (pectin) appear, then the test is positive and a pectolytic enzyme should be used. If there is only a very small amount of pectin present, then instead of strings or clots of pectin you may see only tiny dots of it. Even this small amount of pectin could cause the wine to be cloudy and so a pectin destroying enzyme should still be used. When doing the pectin test, you may also see a sort of translucent milkiness, this is only an effect produced by mixing the meths with the water in the wine, and does *not* indicate the presence of pectin.

Another reason for a wine remaining cloudy is the presence of starch. Once again there is a special enzyme to deal with this, but with the recipes below, a starch haze is most unlikely.

Undoubtedly useful as these enzymes are, it has to be admitted that very little is known about the safety or otherwise of these additives. So to be on the safe side, they should only be used when absolutely essential, and not used routinely as suggested in many home winemaking books. Always bear in mind, that even the haziest of wines which owe their cloudiness to either pectin or starch, will often clear quite spontaneously without the use of enzymes, provided they are stored in a cool place for long enough; this I have proved to my own satisfaction many times. The snag is that 'long enough' may mean a year to 18 months or even longer, so if you drink a lot of wine, storage space could be a limitation.

Finings
Another common cause of cloudiness in wine is the presence of various proteins that come from the fruits and vegetables the wine was made from. These proteins carry minute positive electrical charges when in liquids which are fairly acidic, such as wine. Because of this, the protein particles repel each other (like charges repel, just as similarly charged ends of magnets do) and because they are so physically small, gravity has little effect, so they remain suspended in the wine as a haze. The trick used to eliminate these undesirable particles is to add some negatively charged particles to the wine in the form of finings. Once again, just like magnets, opposite charges attract, and so the charge on the protein particles is neutralized and they are then able to

gravitate to the bottom. The wine is then left clear and bright.

One of the most useful fining agents is a substance known as Bentonite, a special kind of clay which carries the necessary negative charges. Happily, bentonite seems to be one of the safer additives, and so you should have no worries about using it to clear your wines. Fining can sometimes spoil wine by removing not only the haze, but flavour and colour as well, so once again, if possible be patient and give the wine a chance to clear naturally, and never fine it routinely.

Bottling

When your wine is finally clear – and not before – you can bottle it. Always use proper wine bottles, the ones saved from your commercial wine drinking days are ideal. You should also use proper straight sided wine corks, or if you don't intend to keep your wine for long, and don't care about appearance, you can use the horrible reusable plastic stoppers. If you do use proper straight wine corks, you will need to soak them for 24 hours in hot (not boiling) water, keeping them submerged with a teacup or small plate. You will also need a special corking machine to insert them into the bottles, but these are quite inexpensive.

When the wine is crystal clear, siphon it into bottles and seal with corks; use a corking machine and wooden mallet to drive the corks into the bottles.

Once bottled, store your wine in a cool (about 13°C (55°F)) dark place for between six months and a year for light coloured wines, and at least twice this time for red wines. If you use proper wine corks, the bottles *must* be stored on their sides or else the corks will dry out and shrink, so letting in air which will ruin the wine. When using proper corks you should cover the top of the necks with plastic or foil capsules as commercial winemakers do, as this also helps prevent the corks drying out and the consequent loss of wine through seepage. If you use plastic stoppers, the bottles are best stored upright.

The dreaded vinegar fly!

A word of warning, it is important that at all times your wine is protected from insects landing in it as they can often carry bacteria that would be injurious to your wine. In particular, the tiny fruit flies one often sees around decaying fruit can carry a particularly unwelcome type of bacteria which can turn your wine into vinegar; this is why winemakers call these little pests vinegar flies. To keep these little horrors out of harm's way, always make sure your wine is covered with a lid or cloth while being fermented on the pulp. Similarly, while in the demijohn the wine should be sealed at all times with a fermentation trap partly filled with water.

A word about equipment

All the items of equipment needed for making wine – except perhaps the bottles – should be bought from a specialist homebrew shop, or failing that, from the homebrew department of one of the many chain stores now selling winemaking equipment. A basic list of equipment needed to make 4.5 litres (1 gallon) of wine is as follows:

A plastic fermenting bucket with lid – which will hold about 9 litres (2 gallon)
A potato masher (for crushing the ingredients)
A glass 'j' tube for racking
A 1 metre (3 feet) length of rubber (best) or plastic (not so good) tube to attach to the 'j' tube
Two demijohns – one to hold the wine, one to rack into
One air lock (preferably glass) and rubber or cork bung to fit demijohn
A 1 litre (2pt) glass or plastic measuring jug

A large funnel to suit neck of demijohn
A large stainless steel or plastic kitchen sieve
Six wine bottles, corks, capsules and labels – sufficient to
  cope with one gallon of wine
A corking machine

Make certain that none of the equipment that will come into contact with the wine is made of iron, copper, brass, zinc or tin, as the acids in the wine will leach harmful metal salts which might spoil the flavour or appearance of your wine, or could even make it poisonous. All equipment for winemaking must be thoroughly cleaned with hot soapy water and thoroughly rinsed. Beware pouring very hot water into demijohns – they will crack. If your equipment has hard to remove deposits, use either Silana crystals or Chempro, both available from good winemaking shops. Alternatively, a weak solution of household bleach will work just as well.

Yeast and nutrient
The best all-round yeast to use is Formula 67+ which is available from good homebrew shops. Under no circumstances use anything other than wine yeast, certainly never bread yeast, or your wine will be ruined by off-flavours. To ensure rapid and successful fermentations, supplement the yeast nutrients in the Formula 67+ compound with Tronozymol yeast nutrient, again available from good homebrew shops. Add about two level teaspoonfuls to each 4.5 litres (1 gallon) of wine.

RECIPES

Blackcurrant Wine

1.35kg (3lb) blackcurrants
290ml (½pt) red grape concentrate or 450g (1lb) chopped raisins
1.1kg (2¼lb) white sugar
2 teaspoonfuls Tronozymol nutrient
2 teaspoonfuls Formula 67+ yeast compound
3.5 litres (6pt) water

Wash the currants then place them in your bucket and crush well with a potato masher. Add the sugar, grape concentrate or raisins and the water. Stir well to dissolve the sugar, then add the Tronozymol and Formula 67+, stir again, then cover closely with a lid or cloth tied securely round the mouth of the bucket. Ferment on the pulp for seven days, stirring twice daily, then strain into demijohn, fit air lock and continue as directed in basic method (see page 122).

Gooseberry wine

2.7kg (6lb) green gooseberries
290ml (½pt) white grape concentrate (optional)
1kg (2¼lb) white sugar
2 teaspoonfuls Tronozymol nutrient
2 teaspoonfuls Formula 67+ yeast compound
3.5 litres (6pt) water

Wash and top and tail the gooseberries, then 'crack' each berry with a wooden mallet or crush with your hands if the berries are soft enough. Place in your bucket and add the water. Leave to stand for three days keeping well covered and crushing the berries by hand each day. Strain into a demijohn, discard the gooseberries and rinse the bucket out, then put the sugar into it and pour in the liquid from the demijohn. Stir well to dissolve the sugar, then pour back into demijohn and add the grape concentrate, Tronozymol and Formula 67+. Fit airlock and continue as per the basic method (see page 122).

Rhubarb wine

1.35kg (3lb) rhubarb
290ml (½pt) white grape concentrate or 450g (1lb) chopped
  sultanas
1.25kg (2¾lb) sugar
2 teaspoonfuls Tronozymol nutrient
2 teaspoonfuls Formula 67+ yeast compound
water

Wash the rhubarb, cut into 1 cm (½″) lengths and place in your bucket. Pour on the sugar, stir with your hand to mix the rhubarb and sugar together, cover and leave to stand for two days. Strain the liquid into demijohn, then rinse the rhubarb with a little water and strain this into the demijohn also. Repeat until the demijohn is filled to the shoulder. Now add the grape concentrate, Tronozymol and Formula 67+. Fit airlock and continue as for the basic method (see page 122).

If using sultanas instead of grape concentrate, strain the liquid off the rhubarb into a bucket, rinsing the rhubarb with water as before, collecting about 4.5 litres (1 gallon) of liquid in all. Now add the chopped sultanas and the yeast and nutrient and stir well. Cover closely and ferment on the pulp for five days stirring twice a day. Strain into a demijohn and continue as before.

Strawberry wine

1.8kg (4lb) ripe strawberries
juice of 4 large oranges
290ml (½pt) red grape concentrate or 450g (1lb) chopped
   raisins
1kg (2¼lb) sugar
2 teaspoonfuls Tronozymol nutrient
2 teaspoonfuls Formula 67+ yeast compound
3.5 litres (6pt) water

Wash and hull the strawberries, place in your bucket and crush well with your fingers. Add the sugar, stir well, then cover the bucket and leave to stand for twelve hours. Now add the water, the grape concentrate or raisins, the orange juices, the yeast and nutrient. Stir well and then cover and leave to ferment on the pulp for five days, stirring twice a day. Strain into demijohn, topping up to the bottom of the neck as necessary. Continue as directed in the basic method (see page 122).

Dried fig wine

900g (2lb) dried figs
juice of 2 lemons
juice of 2 oranges
290ml (½pt) white grape concentrate or 450g (1lb) chopped
   sultanas
1kg (2¼lb) white sugar
110g (4oz) genuine Muscavado sugar
2 teaspoonfuls Tronozymol nutrient
2 teaspoonfuls Formula 67+ yeast compound
4.5 litres (1 gallon) water

Chop the figs and place in bucket, add the white sugar and pour on 4.5 litres (1 gallon) water. Add the grape concentrate or sultanas, the lemon and orange juices and the yeast and nutrient. Stir well and allow to ferment for nine days, keeping the bucket well covered and stirring twice a day. Strain into demijohn and add the Muscavado sugar, giving the demijohn a good shake to dissolve it. Top up if required and continue in the usual way (see page 122).

Apricot melomel

One of my favourites!

560g (1¼lb) honey
290ml (½pt) white grape concentrate or 450g (1lb) chopped
  sultanas
450g (1lb) chopped dried apricots
15g (½oz) malic acid
8g (¼oz) citric acid
2 teaspoonfuls Tronozymol nutrient
2 teaspoonfuls Formula 67+ yeast compound
4.5 litres (1 gallon) water

Dissolve the honey in 4.5 litres (1 gallon) cold water. When dissolved, add the grape concentrate or chopped sultanas and the apricots. Add the malic acid and the yeast and nutrient. Stir well and allow to ferment for seven days keeping closely covered, stirring twice a day. Strain into demijohn, top up to bottom of neck, and continue as usual (see page 122).

Elderflower champagne

This isn't really a 'wine' at all, but a refreshing sparkling drink of very low alcohol content, and is deliciously thirst quenching on hot summer days – especially if chilled in the fridge beforehand. This recipe is not my own, but was given to me by a Mr Allen, a wonderful man whom I met in Norfolk one glorious summer while still in my teens.

2–4 elder florets
2 tablespoonfuls white wine vinegar
juice and grated rind* of a lemon
560g (1¼lb) sugar
4.5 litres (1 gallon) water

*In view of the fungicides used on the skins of lemons and other citrus fruits for that matter, it would be wiser not to use the rind at all. Just use the juice.

Gather the elder florets on a warm sunny day when the flowers are fully open. Place the florets in your bucket together with the sugar and pour on the boiling water. Stir well, cover and leave to cool. When cool, add the rest of the ingredients and stir well. Cover the bucket and leave for 24 hours stirring twice during this time. Strain into strong screw top bottles, filling to within about two or three inches of the top, and screw the lids down firmly. Store outside in a cool place for 14 days before drinking. If possible serve chilled – transfer the bottles to the fridge the day before drinking.

Since pressure will build up in the bottles during storage, there is a slight chance that a bottle may burst. Although this happens only *very* rarely, to be on the safe side, store the bottles outside in a cool place out of the sun, and handle them very carefully, and never hold a bottle near your face. For the same reason, aim to drink it all within a few weeks – it is not suitable for long-term keeping.

10.
ICE CREAM

Quite simply most ice cream on sale in shops is a con. As far as British laws are concerned, a food company can make a product that doesn't contain a single drop of cream and still quite legally sell it as ice cream. This deception has not gone unnoticed by the EEC, and there are several countries that would like to see our erroneous use of the term ice cream outlawed.

The reason for the reluctance of the food industry to use cream is as you would expect – because it's expensive. What's used instead, is cheap, low-grade vegetable oil, which is available to the industry in abundance. To make this rubbish emulate some of the physical properties of real cream, they have to doctor it with various chemical additives in the form of emulsifiers and stabilizers. Even the so called 'dairy' ice creams sold in Britain are not quite what they seem. Admittedly they contain only dairy fat rather than vegetable oil, but the minimum amount they must contain is a paltry five per cent; even the economy ice cream recipes later in this chapter contain more than twice that amount, and yet these commercially produced 'dairy' ice creams are marketed as luxury foods with prices to match.

As well as the emulsifiers and stabilizers, there are also the artificial flavourings and colourings to contend with. Many ice creams contain colourings like tartrazine E102, sunset yellow E110 and amaranth E123, all of which belong to a group of chemicals called azo dyes which are known to provoke various general intolerance reactions and cause hyperactivity in children. And as for flavourings, well who knows what they use – certainly not the buying public – since the industry can get away with putting any flavouring chemical it likes into our food and doesn't have to declare what it uses to anyone except a select group of civil servants who are sworn to secrecy. If you make your own ice cream, not only will you have a far tastier product, you can also be confident that it doesn't contain chemicals that may be injurious to your health.

HOMEMADE ICE CREAM

There are two approaches to making ice cream, and which one you choose depends on how cost and calorie conscious you feel. The more extravagant method is to use all cream, and this makes the richest and most delicious ice creams, products which really are what their name suggests: iced cream. A more economical way is to substitute a proportion of custard for some of the cream. Ice creams made in this way are not so rich, but because they contain less fat are healthier and easier to digest.

Whichever way you choose to make your ice cream, the basic method is the same. What you must do, having prepared your cream or cream and custard mixture, is freeze it in such a way that only *small* ice crystals form. This ensures that it has a nice soft texture and doesn't just freeze into a solid unyielding lump. The first thing you need then, is some method of freezing your ice cream. This usually means using a deep freeze or the ice box of a refrigerator. There are however ice cream making machines that have their own refrigeration systems built in, and so don't need to be placed inside a fridge or freezer, but these cost hundreds of pounds to buy, and are really only worth considering if you intend to make ice cream in a big way. With cheaper machines, like the one I have, you simply put the whole contraption in your ice box or freezer and let it get on with it. Irrespective of how sophisticated they are, all ice cream machines work on the principle that provided you continually stir the ice cream mixture as it freezes, large ice crystals cannot form; they are nothing more than automatic low temperature stirring devices. It is possible to make ice cream without an ice cream machine, and although more laborious, the results are usually nearly as good. A full description of how to do this follows below.

RECIPES

Chocolate or Carob Ice Cream

This recipe uses a custard base to reduce the amount of cream needed.

425ml (¾pt) milk
3 eggs
290ml (½pt) chilled double cream
1 tablespoon honey
225g (8oz) plain chocolate*

*If you prefer to avoid the caffeine and sugar in chocolate, use bars of unsweetened carob 'chocolate' available from wholefood shops instead.

Beat the eggs with a tablespoon of the milk. Heat the remaining milk in a saucepan until it is hand hot and then pour onto the beaten eggs beating well. Now heat this custard mixture in a double saucepan until it *just* starts to thicken. As soon as the custard thickens, stop heating it or it will curdle. If you haven't got a double saucepan, you can make the custard in an ordinary pan, but heat it very slowly and stir it continuously. On no account let the custard boil or it will be ruined.

Having made the custard, add the honey and stir well until fully dissolved, then stand the pan in a sink of cold water and allow it to cool, giving it an occasional stir. While the custard is cooling, break the chocolate or carob bar into small pieces and place in a heat proof bowl. Stand the bowl over a pan of boiling water and allow the chocolate to melt, giving it a stir from time to time. If the chocolate is a little stiff, add a couple of tablespoons of milk to thin it out.

As soon as the chocolate has melted, add it to the custard and stir it in well. If after adding the chocolate the custard is still warm, stand it in the sink for a little longer until completely cold before proceeding to the next stage. Meanwhile, whip the cream lightly until it *just* starts to thicken, then fold it into the cold custard. On no account add the cream to warm custard or the texture of the ice cream will be spoiled.

What you do next depends on whether you have an ice cream machine or not. If you have, simply pour the prepared mixture into it and follow the manufacturers instructions. If you haven't got a special machine, pour the ice cream mixture into a wide, shallow tray or bowl, and put it into either your deep freeze or refrigerator ice box. If you are using a fridge rather than a deep freeze, turn it up to the maximum setting. Leave the ice cream for about half an hour then take it out and beat it thoroughly. Return to the fridge or freezer and leave for twenty minutes then take it out and beat it again. Continue chilling and beating the ice cream at twenty minute intervals until it becomes too stiff to beat. At this point the ice cream should be packed into whatever container you intend to store it in and put back into the ice box or deep freeze to finish freezing. Make sure the container is chilled beforehand and transfer the ice cream as swiftly as possible so that it doesn't melt. If you prefer, the ice cream can simply be left in the container you made it in. In a deep freeze ice cream should keep for at least four months, but if stored in a refrigerator ice box it should be eaten within a few days or a week at the most. Be sure to cover the ice cream tightly or put it in a polythene bag or else it will dry out in storage.

Yield: about 950ml (1½pt).

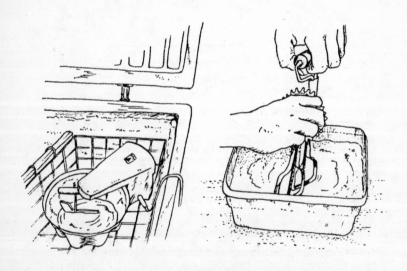

Ice cream should be frozen in a shallow tray and beaten every twenty minutes. An easier method is to use an ice cream machine which stirs the ice cream continuously as it freezes.

Vanilla Ice Cream

425ml (³/₄pt) milk
3 eggs
290ml (¹/₂pt) chilled double cream
2 tablespoons honey
1 large vanilla pod cut in half lengthwise or 1 teaspoonful
  vanilla essence

Heat the milk to just below boiling then add the vanilla pod.
Cover the pan with a lid and leave to stand for half an hour
to allow the pod to flavour the milk. Remove the vanilla pod
from the milk, reheat the milk to hand hot and make the
custard exactly as in the previous recipe. When the custard
has cooled, whip the cream lightly and fold into the custard.
If you are using vanilla essence instead of pod vanilla, this
should be added now. Freeze, beating periodically as for
chocolate ice cream (see page 135).

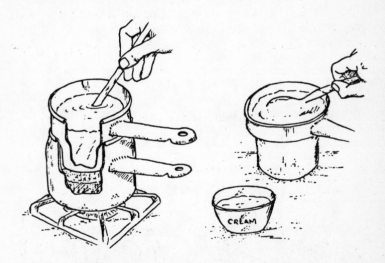

Once the custard has thickened, place the pan in a sinkful of cold
water to cool it. When cool, fold in the lightly whipped cream.

   As an economy measure, the vanilla pod can be reused;
simply wash the milk off it well and hang it up to dry.
Within a couple of hours the pod will have dried sufficiently
to be stored in a small airtight jar until next time. After
using the pod a second time discard it.
   Yield: about 950ml (1¹/₂pt).

Tutti-Frutti Ice Cream

425ml (¾pt) milk
3 eggs
290ml (½pt) chilled double cream
2 tablespoonfuls honey
1 large vanilla pod or 1 teaspoonful vanilla essence
55g (2oz) finely chopped glacé cherries
55g (2oz) seedless raisins
55g (2oz) sultanas
85g (3oz) mixed candied peel
small glass of rum (optional, but nice!)

Make a vanilla ice cream mixture (see page 137) using the
first five ingredients. Before freezing, stir in the fruit and
rum and then freeze in the usual way (see page 135). To add
a little extra luxury, soak the raisins and sultanas in rum
the night before making the ice cream.
     Yield: about 1 litre (1¾pt).

Coffee Ice Cream

425ml (¾pt) milk
3 eggs
290ml (½pt) chilled double cream
3 tablespoonfuls honey
5 level teaspoonfuls instant coffee* dissolved in 2
     tablespoonfuls boiling water or 145ml (¼pt) very strong
     black coffee

*If you prefer not to use coffee, use a similar amount of one
of the many coffee substitutes available from wholefood
shops.

As usual, use the eggs and milk to make a custard (see page
135). When cool, stir in the coffee and fold in the whipped
cream. The mixture should then be frozen as usual (see page
135).
     Yield: about 950ml (1½pt).

Fruit Ice Cream

425ml (¾pt) milk
3 eggs
290ml (½pt) chilled double cream
2–3 tablespoonfuls honey

225g (8oz) soft fruit e.g. raspberries, blackcurrants,
   strawberries

Make a basic ice cream mixture (see page 135) using the
milk, eggs, cream and honey. Puree the fruit by either using
a rotary sieve or a liquidizer. If you use the latter, add a
couple of tablespoons milk to the fruit before liquidizing. Stir
the pureed fruit into the ice cream mixture and freeze (see
page 135).
   Yield: about 1 litre (1¾pt).

Ice Creams for Special Occasions

Once in a while it does us all good to be a little extravagant.
So if you feel it's time you had a little treat, have a go at
making ice cream made only with cream and not spanned
out with custard. This sort of ice cream is delicious beyond
words, but sadly contains so much fat that it can hardly be
described as healthy eating, and strictly speaking has no
place in a book about making healthy foods! However, as an
occasional treat I'm sure its nutritional shortcomings can be
overlooked. Any of the recipes on pages 135 to 139 can be
adapted by simply substituting 1½pt of double cream for the
first three ingredients in each recipe. To make the ice cream,
all you have to do is to whip the cream until it just starts to
thicken, then add the appropriate flavouring and the honey
which should first be dissolved in a couple of tablespoons of
hot milk. In the case of the vanilla ice cream recipe (page
137), you should either use vanilla essence or flavour the
honey with vanilla pods. Do this by cutting three vanilla
pods in half length ways and adding them to a 450g (1lb) jar
of liquid honey. Keep this in a warm place for a month or so
and you will have a supply of vanilla flavoured honey which
is useful not only for making vanilla ice cream, but all sorts
of dessert dishes.

SERVING ICE CREAM

Before serving, take the ice cream out of the fridge or freezer
and stand it in a cool place for 30 minutes to an hour to
allow the ice cream to soften slightly.

11.
ORGANIC
HERB
GROWING

A great many of the recipes in this book call for the use of
herbs in one way or another. Although many of us will have
to make do with dried herbs, it is always far better to use
fresh herbs as these have a much finer and more pungent
flavour.

Unfortunately, finding fresh herbs when you want them
isn't easy, and the best solution is to grow your own.
Growing your own herbs is also a great money saver, since
when you can actually find fresh herbs for sale, they are
usually rather expensive, and will invariably be past their
best by the time you come to use them.

All the previous chapters have been about making foods
that don't contain dubious additives and large amounts of
salt and sugar. In just the same way as it is possible to
produce foods without additives, so it is possible to grow
crops without highly toxic pesticides, using only natural
measures and composts. Food produced in this way is said to
be organically grown. Organically grown crops not only taste
better, they are more nutritious and are also more resistant
to pests and diseases. It would require a whole book the size
of this one to cover in adequate detail the various techniques
and systems of organic gardening. All I can do here is
scratch the surface, but enough I hope, to whet your appetite
to find out more from the books listed at the end of the
chapter. Even so, you should still find enough information to
start you off growing herbs organically.

PRACTICAL HERB GROWING

Growing a few culinary herbs in your own garden is simple

and straightforward and requires no expensive special equipment. One of the cheapest ways to raise herbs is by seed. To do this you certainly won't need a greenhouse or a fancy heated propagator. A warm windowsill is all that's required.

A more expensive way of getting fresh herbs is to buy them ready grown in little pots from nurseries and garden centres. The advantage with this method though, is that you have your herbs immediately, although you will have to wait for the plants to establish themselves and grow large enough before you can start tearing bits off to use. Provided you only want a small number of herb plants, buying them pot-grown needn't work out too expensive. It can represent a good investment when you consider that the plants will supply your needs for many years to come – provided of course that you only buy perennials. Never waste money buying annual or biennial herbs in this way, as these will only live for one or two years respectively, before flowering and dying. The best way to grow annual or biennial herbs is by raising them from seed.

Some herbs can be propagated from cuttings of one sort or another, or by dividing up large well-established clumps into smaller pieces which regrow with renewed vigour. If you know someone who already has an established herb garden, then propagation from cuttings or division is a way of acquiring your herbs for free. In fact there is much to commend propagating herbs by these (vegetative) methods rather than by seed which relies on the sexual process of pollination, and often produces plants which are not genetically identical to the parent plant. What this means in practice, is that herbs grown from seed can sometimes be rather less pungent, or have a slightly different flavour or aroma than expected. With vegetative propagation from cuttings or division, the new plants produced are genetically identical to the donor plant, and so if *it* has a nice strong, aromatic flavour, so will the new plants. Always make sure the plant you divide or take cuttings from really does have a good flavour and aroma. Also bear this in mind when buying pot-grown herbs.

CHOOSING COMPOST

Whether you grow your herbs from seed or from cuttings, you will need special compost to grow them in during their early stages of development. Choose your compost carefully as some brands are definitely better than others. For example, the great majority of commercially mixed John Innes composts are very poor indeed, despite the excellence of the basic John Innes formula. The trouble is that the high quality loam needed to mix these composts is very rare and expensive nowadays. Consequently, these formerly excellent composts tend to lack any of the structure essential for holding air and moisture, and tend to dry out rapidly, and once dry, are very difficult to re-wet. This shortage of loam with which to make these soil-based composts has led to the increasing popularity of soil-less peat based composts of which the Levington composts are typical. These too are problematic, as they tend to hold rather too much water, with the inevitable result that seeds and roots can easily be rotted by over watering. I have found the best way round these difficulties with both sorts of compost is to mix them together in equal volumes. A mixture of equal parts John Innes No2 and Levington potting compost makes a first rate compost for general use.

Organic composts
The trouble with orthodox composts such as the John Innes and Levington types already mentioned, is that they contain artificial fertilizers. Artificial fertilizers are harmful wherever they are used, whether that be on a thousand acre cereal prairie, or in your own back yard – you only have to look at the rising levels of dangerous nitrates in our water supplies (largely from the leaching and run-off of nitrogenous artificial fertilizers) to see that.

Happily, over the last few years, organic alternatives to conventional composts have become available. Although they are not yet that easy to obtain, they are available and if at all possible you should use them. A good, sensibly priced one is marketed under the name of 'Cowpost', and is clean and pleasant to use despite its name. However, I have found that like peat-based composts, it easily becomes waterlogged, and when it dries out, in common with most John Innes composts, it is difficult to re-wet. To improve matters, mix one part of potting grit to every two parts of Cowpost. If your local garden centre or shop doesn't sell Cowpost, or one of the other organic composts, ask them to stock it, or if that doesn't work, write direct to the makers (see page 159) for your nearest stockist, or order it from them direct. Plants grown organically are stronger and more disease resistant and taste better as well, so it is well worth the trouble to use organic methods and opt for genuine organic composts right from the start of a plant's life.

TECHNIQUES OF PROPAGATION

There are many ways for the gardener to propagate plants, some techniques will only work for certain plants, whereas others have a more general application. What follows below is a brief guide to the techniques most often used to propagate herbs in my own garden, and is followed by a more detailed description of the propagation and use of eighteen popular herbs.

By seed

Annual and biennial herbs are always grown from seed. You can also grow most of the perennial sorts this way too. All you need to raise herbs from seed, apart from the seed itself of course, is a seed tray, some compost to sow the seeds in, and something to cover the tray with to stop the compost drying out while the seeds germinate. It is possible to buy seed trays with transparent plastic covers especially for the job, but an ordinary seed tray placed in a large plastic bag would do nearly as well.

When you are ready to sow your seeds, fill the seed tray with compost and firm it down gently using a block of wood. Now, with a pencil, make holes in the compost about ¼ inch deep and about 1½ inches apart. In these holes sow the seeds thinly, and then using a finger, push the compost back into the holes to cover the seeds. Remember to label each hole, so you know which seeds are where; an old plastic bottle cut into strips makes good push-in markers. When you have sown your seeds, water the compost *gently* using a watering can with a *fine* rose. If this isn't done carefully you will wash the seeds out of the compost. If you haven't got a suitable watering can, stand the tray in a bowl of water and let the compost soak the water up.

Very small seeds, for example those of the mints, should not be buried in the compost. Instead water the tray of compost well and then simply sprinkle the seeds on the damp surface.

If you are using one of the special propagating trays with a transparent plastic cover, you should cover the tray with this and close off any ventilation holes there may be in the lid. Otherwise, just put the whole tray in a plastic bag and tie it closed. You should stand the tray on a warm windowsill, and if it catches direct sunlight, cover it with a piece of newspaper to prevent the compost from overheating. If you neglect to do this, the temperature of the compost will, on sunny days, quickly rise to a level that will either kill, or at least damage the germinating seeds.

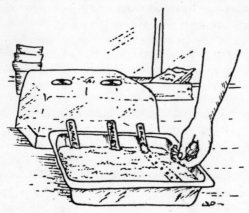

Sow herb seeds in a tray of compost on a warm windowsill, remembering to label each row.

After what may be up to several weeks with some varieties of herb, you should begin to see the first leaves of the young plants emerging from the compost. At this point you should give some ventilation, either by opening the polythene bag or by opening the vents on the plastic propagator cover. You should also see that the seedlings get plenty of light, but still guard them from fierce direct sunlight until they have hardened up a little.

As soon as the seedlings have their first leaves (or leaf) fully unfurled they should be transplanted or *pricked out*. Before doing this, give the compost a light sprinkling with water to soften it. Now gently lift out the seedling using the handle of a teaspoon or something similar, being careful to ensure that as much compost remains round the roots as possible. Always handle the seedlings by their leaves *not* by their stalks which are easily damaged. Transfer the seedlings to 3 inch pots of compost, placing one seedling in the centre of each pot. Firm the compost *gently* around the roots and then water the little plants well. The plants should be allowed to continue to grow on the windowsill and watered only when the compost feels dry.

You can continue to grow your herbs indoors if you have no other option, but they will be far more productive and live much longer if you can transfer them to your garden outside as soon as they begin to outgrow their pots. Before doing this, you must gradually accustom the as yet, rather tender and cosseted little plants, to the harsher conditions they must contend with in the great outdoors. This gradual acclimatization process is called *hardening-off* and is best achieved by placing the plants in a sheltered but sunny spot out of doors on every fine warm day. The plants should b e brought back in again at night for the first two or three weeks after which they can be left outside permanently, provided the nights are not too windy or cold. As a general rule, you should not be thinking about hardening off your plants until early summer. Be especially vigilant with tender or half-hardy plants as these are easily killed or can have their growth checked if put outside too soon.

As soon as your herb plants are fully hardened off, you can transfer them to their permanent sites. Most will grow quite happily in pots of compost on a patio or balcony if you have nowhere else for them, but they will do better if planted into open soil. If you choose to grow them in pots, use pots at least 8 inches in diameter.

Cuttings

There are many different ways of taking cuttings from perennial plants, but the most useful techniques for herbs are *hardwood* and *semi-hardwood* cuttings. Of the two, hardwood cuttings are the easiest to do. To take a hardwood cutting you should go to your plant in late winter and pull a piece of stem off it with a downward tug, so as to leave a piece of the main stem attached, this piece of main stem is known as a *heel*. Now shorten the cutting to about 4 inches long by trimming some of the top off with a sharp knife just above a bud. Your cuttings should be pushed in (heel end down) round the edge of a pot filled with a mixture of one part of your usual compost and one part of potting grit. The pot of cuttings should then be left in a sheltered spot out of doors and in the spring the cuttings should begin to grow.

As soon as the cuttings have started to grow and have good root systems, the cuttings can be separated and each one placed in its own pot – this is called *potting-up*. After

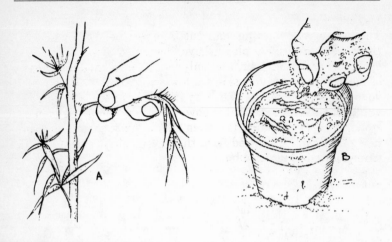

A. *To take a cutting, first pull a piece of stem off the parent plant so as to leave a heel attached.*

B. *To propagate from root cuttings, cut short sections of fairly thick root from the donor plant and bury them in pots of compost. When the new plants appear they can be potted-up singly.*

potting-up, the plants should then be allowed to continue growing, and as soon as they are large enough, transfer them to their permanent sites, whether that be in open soil or large pots of compost.

Semi-hardwood cuttings are taken during the summer when the new season's growth is just starting to harden off. You can either pull a piece of stem off with a heel as for hardwood cuttings, or alternatively, cut a piece of stem off just below a leaf joint. You should then remove all the leaves from the lower third of the cuttings, shorten the cuttings to about 4 inches long by trimming the tops just above a bud, and then place them round the edge of a pot of grit enriched compost as you would a hardwood cutting. This time however, the pot of cuttings, after being watered well, should be placed in a plastic bag to prevent the cuttings drying out. The cuttings should be kept on a warm windowsill and protected from direct sunlight. As soon as the cuttings develop good root systems and start growing, you should pot them up individually, and when well established, harden them off and plant outside.

Layering

This is a way of making your cuttings root before you sever them from the parent plant. Layering is best done in the spring or early summer, and only works with shrubby types of herb. What you do is select a low-lying stem of the herb you want to propagate, and bury part of it in the soil; you will probably need to hold it down with a wooden peg or a stone. By early autumn the stem should have rooted and the new plant can be severed from the parent plant and transplanted to its new home.

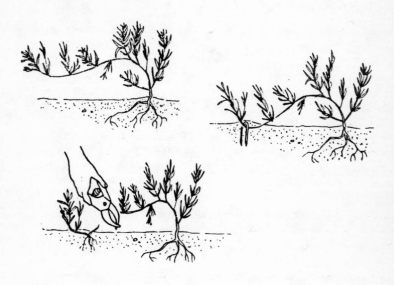

Layering: Bury a low branch of the plant in the soil, holding it in place with a stone, wooden peg or piece of bent wire. When the new plant has rooted it should be severed from the main plant.

Root cuttings

These should be taken when the plant is dormant during the winter or early spring. All you need to do is cut off small pieces from the more substantial roots of the parent plant and bury them horizontally about an inch deep in pots of compost. Alternatively, plant them directly where you want the new plants to grow.

Division

Division should be done in the spring and autumn, and simply entails digging up a large well established clump of whatever you want to propagate, and then breaking it into several smaller pieces which you immediately replant. Having dug the plant up, you can divide it up either with a spade or by teasing it apart with a fork, or for a very dense clump, by prizing it apart with two forks used back to back.

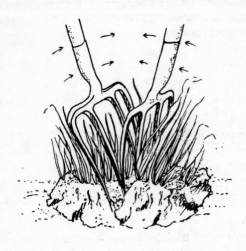

Division: Plunge two forks into the clump to be divided back to back, then draw the handles together to lever the clump apart.

HERBS ONE BY ONE

Angelica *(Angelica archangelica)*

Biennial

This is a really enormous herb: some of the plants I have raised have grown in excess of 7 feet high and have had a spread of something like 5 feet! Clearly this is not a herb for a small garden! If you do have room for it, it likes a somewhat shady spot with good rich soil and plenty of moisture. It is propagated by seed, which should be sown either outside or on a warm windowsill in the early spring. Germination can take a long time, so be patient. Unfortunately, the seeds don't keep for long, so unless you can be sure your seed is from the previous season, it is a good idea to buy a plant initially, and use the seeds that it produces to provide further generations of plants. Angelica is nominally a biennial, but will often live for longer than two years before it finally flowers and dies.

The stems are the most often used part of the plant. These can be candied or used to flavour liqueurs and cordials, or stewed with rhubarb to reduce its tartness. The leaves are also valuable and can be used to make a tisane which is good for the relief of digestive problems. The roots may also be used in a similar manner.

Angelica Liqueur

Combine 30g (1oz) of chopped fresh angelica stem, 30g (1oz) of skinned and chopped bitter almonds, 140g (5oz) honey and a bottle of cheap brandy in a large jar and leave for seven days giving the jar a shake each day. Strain through fine muslin and bottle. The liqueur is best kept for a few months before drinking.

Bay *(Laurus nobilis)*

Perennial

This is a shrubby perennial herb renowned for its aromatic leaves which are usually dried before use. You must always remember that although bay looks very hardy, it isn't, and frost will quickly kill it. The best thing to do is grow it in a pot and bring it into a cool room for the winter. During the summer it likes to be in a nice sunny place. Bay can be propagated by either hardwood or semi-hardwood cuttings. In the kitchen the leaves can be used to flavour all manner of savoury dishes from stews to curries, and are also very good to add to jars of pickles.

Chervil *(Anthriscus cerefolium)*

Biennial

This herb, from a culinary point of view at least, is really a superior type of parsley. It can be used in exactly the same way as parsley, but has a far finer flavour. Ideally, chervil should be sown repeatedly from early spring to early autumn to ensure a continuous supply of fresh leaves. Chervil will even stand into the winter if given some protection. It is often claimed that chervil does not like to be transplanted and so must be sown in situ outside, but I have never had any problems raising it in seed trays like other herbs.

Chives *(Allium schoenoprasum)*

Perennial

Chives are a sort of perennial green onion, and are both easy
to grow and very prolific producers of delicious onion
flavoured leaves. Provided chives have plenty of moisture
and are given some shade, they are not at all fussy about
soil. Although they can be raised from seed sown indoors in
the spring, the best way to propagate them is by division of
an established clump.

Chives provide a delicious way of perking up the flavour of
soft cheeses, and are particularly nice chopped up in salads.

Dill *(Anethum graveolens)*

Annual

Both the seeds and leaves of dill can be used, but the seeds
are far more pungent. The seeds are claimed to have a
calming effect, and in fact its common name is derived from
the Norse word *dilla* which means to lull. Being an annual,
it must be grown each year from seed, and like chervil is
best sown in succession for a continuous supply, starting
indoors in early spring. Because dill is very closely related to
fennel (see page below), you must not grow them both in the
same garden if you want to use the seeds to propagate more
plants, since dill and fennel readily cross pollinate each
other to produce undesirable hybrids. If you don't care about
the seeds or only want them for culinary use, it doesn't
matter.

Dill leaves are especially pleasant with white fish, and can
also be used to add a pleasant aromatic flavour to sausages
and burgers. The seeds can be used as part of a pickling
spice mixture and are traditionally used in large amounts
with pickled cucumbers.

Fennel *(Foeniculum vulgare)*

Perennial

This is often confused with Florence fennel (*F. dulce*) which
is usually grown as a vegetable, whereas the ordinary
variety (*F. vulgare*) is grown for its aromatic leaves. Fennel
is quite similar to dill both in appearance and flavour,
although fennel has a sweeter flavour more reminiscent of
anise. Like dill, fennel goes well with fish and can be used to

give a lift to all sorts of savoury dishes.

Propagation is by seed which should be sown on a warm windowsill in early spring, or alternatively, well established plants can be divided with a sharp spade in the autumn or early spring. If you want to use the seeds from your own plants to raise further plants, you must not grow dill as well – see page 150.

Hyssop *(Hyssopus officienalis)*

Perennial

Hyssop, like dill and fennel, is a most distinctive and aromatic herb, and is useful in all kinds of savoury meat and fish based dishes, especially the more fatty sorts. Provided it is not too wet, hyssop is not over fussy about soil, although it likes light well-drained soil best. To do well it should be grown in a spot where it will get plenty of sun. In the winter its roots are particularly prone to rotting if it is grown in wet soil, so ensure adequate drainage, or else grow it in a large pot and shelter it from the winter rains. Propagation is by seed or by hardwood or semi-hardwood cuttings.

Lemon Balm *(Melissa officianalis)*

Perennial

Lemon Balm is a most attractive herb with deliciously lemon scented leaves that can be used to flavour drinks and puddings, and make a delicious summer tisane. Propagation is by seed sown in the spring on a warm windowsill, or by division in the autumn or spring. Choose a site that has good rich soil which is moist but not wet, and where it will get some shade, as it doesn't like the fierce summer sun.

Lovage *(Ligusticum officianalis)*

Perennial

This herb can grow quite large given ideal conditions, although nothing like the size angelica can achieve. Given a deep moisture retentive soil, with plenty of compost or manure, lovage will be quite happy. Although often recommended as an addition to stews and soups, I prefer to use its leaves chopped up in soft cheeses and salads. Lovage can be grown either from seed or by dividing a well established clump. If you choose to propagate by division, make sure each piece of root has a bud or 'eye' at the top.

Mint *(Mentha spp)*

Perennial

There are many different species and varieties of mint, but the best sort to grow if you only have room to grow one variety is Bowles mint (*M. rotundifolia*, var Bowles). This has nice bulky leaves that make superb mint sauce. Mint also makes a refreshing tisane, and can be added to summer desserts to lend a refreshing coolness. Mint is best propagated by root cutting but can also be grown from seed.

Parsley *(Petroselinum crispum)*

Biennial

This must surely be the most widely known and used of all the culinary herbs, and everyone who has a garden should grow this magnificent herb. Being a biennial, parsley should be raised from seed sown on a warm windowsill in the early spring. Be patient as the seed can take quite a long time to germinate, so keep an eye on the compost to make sure it doesn't dry out in the meantime.

If you can give the plants some protection you will have fresh parsley all through the winter, provided the weather isn't too severe. The following summer the plants will flower and die, but by that time your new plants will have started production. Parsley is a universally useful herb for enhancing the flavour of all kinds of savoury food.

Pot Marjoram *(Origanum onites)*

Perennial

This is the most commonly grown type of marjoram and is a hardy perennial that thrives in pots as well as in the open soil. This is one of the most versatile herbs you can grow, and can be used to flavour everything from sausages and burgers to salads and soft cheeses. Marjoram will grow in most soils and likes plenty of sun. You can propagate it from seed, cuttings or by division.

Rosemary *(Rosmarinus officianalis)*

Perennial

Rosemary has a pervasive resinous flavour and aroma that compliments fatty meats well. If you enjoy barbecuing during the summer months, try burning a branch of rosemary on the charcoal to add extra flavour to the food. A sprig placed on top of a joint of lamb before roasting adds a delicious piquancy: add plenty to pork sausages as it seems to offset any greasiness.

Rosemary is a shrubby herb that likes to grow in full sun in a soil that is light and well drained, although it will grow in any soil provided it isn't too wet. You will have to add some lime if your soil is at all acidic. Propagation is by seed, or better, by cuttings or layering. In the winter the plants are best protected from severe frosts with straw or leaves, or else they may not survive. If you regularly get very cold winters it might be safer to grow rosemary in pots and bring it into a cool room for the winter.

Sage *(Salvia officianalis)*

Perennial

There are two main types of sage: narrow leaved and broad leaved. Of the two, narrow leaved sage is the most commonly grown sort, and is the one I grow myself. Although this is a perennial herb, after a few years the plants begin to lose vigour and should be replaced by new plants grown from cuttings or by layering. It is also possible to grow sage from seed. Sage can be added to savoury food of all types and like rosemary, lends itself well to fatty or greasy meats, so making it an ideal sausage herb.

Sweet Basil *(Ocimum basilicum)*

Annual

Strictly speaking basil is a perennial, but in our temperate climate it must be considered as a half-hardy annual. Basil simply will not grow unless it is kept warm and sheltered – I always grow mine in my greenhouse with the tomatoes. It likes light free-draining soil, but it will tolerate most soils provided they aren't too wet. You should grow basil from seed each year sowing the seed in a warm place in early spring. When the plants are about six inches tall start pinching the tips out to make the plants bushy. Always keep them indoors until you are sure summer has arrived.

The leaves have a unique and powerful pungency that goes well with salads and tomato dishes, and also helps to liven up pork sausages.

Tarragon *(Artemesia dracunculus)*

Perennial

There are two types of tarragon, both perennials, the more flavoursome being the French variety. The Russian sort is nowhere near as good, and to my mind isn't worth growing. To ensure you end up with the superior French kind, it is advisable to propagate from an established plant by division or root cuttings. Tarragon prefers a sunny aspect and a light, not too rich, dry soil, with perhaps a little lime added. It will however grow quite happily in most soils. As winter approaches, cut the dead or dying stalks down to ground level and mulch with straw or leaves to keep the worst of the frost off it.

Tarragon is a good flavouring for savoury sauces and is used a great deal in French cookery. You can make your own tarragon vinegar by stuffing a large sprig into a bottle of cider or white wine vinegar and leaving it to steep for a couple of months.

Thyme *(Thymus vulgaris)*

Perennial

This small leaved, straggly herb, has many different varieties, including the very attractive golden thyme. However, for flavour and general hardiness, the common green thyme is the best choice. Thyme is a perennial and can be grown from seed, cuttings, by layering or division. Choose a sunny well drained site for best results. Although it isn't too particular, light but fertile soil suits it best. If you are short of room in your herb garden, thyme looks very attractive as part of an ornamental rockery. Thyme is a very versatile herb and can be used to flavour stuffings, stocks and stews, and is a good one to add to meat cures. It also tastes good in sausages and burgers.

Winter Savory *(Satureia montana)*

Perennial

Unlike summer savory, winter savory is a hardy perennial herb. If possible, grow it on well drained light soil in full sun, but it will grow well on all but the heaviest soils provided they are not too wet. Savory is sometimes called the bean herb since if you add a sprig to your beans while they are boiling, it really brings their flavour out. Savory is also a good herb to flavour soups and stocks with.

You can propagate savory from cuttings, by layering or from seed.

ORGANIC SOIL MANAGEMENT

The soil is a complex living entity in its own right, and so must be fed and nurtured just as any living thing must be. The plants we grow in the soil are part of this teeming vibrant community. Nutrients which the plant needs are produced as a natural by-product of the life functions of the soil and the organisms that live in it. Not surprisingly then, a healthy 'living' soil will grow healthy plants, which are more resistant to pests and diseases (and usually taste better). Our soil cannot be healthy if it is fed a diet of artificial fertilizers, no more than we can be healthy if we live on junk food. And as conventional chemical-based agriculture has proved, an unhealthy soil grows unhealthy crops which need to be constantly 'drugged' with pesticides if they are to survive at all.

In practice, organic soil management means feeding the soil with healthy food in the form of vegetable and animal wastes. These are usually not added directly as they are, but in the form of manures and composts. There is sadly not room here to explain how to make composts and explain the pros and cons of various manures. For further details you must consult one of the books listed at the end of the chapter (see page 157). Always remember this fundamental natural cycle: the soil feeds the plants, the plants feed us, and we feed the soil.

ORGANIC PEST CONTROL

Even organically grown plants can get pest problems from time to time, so it is as well to know how to deal with them when they arise. The most likely pests to attack your herbs are aphids and caterpillars, although slugs and snails can often be quite troublesome. Fortunately, all of these pests can be easily, and more importantly *safely* dealt with by organic methods.

Aphids
This includes green fly, black fly and all the other so called

sap-sucking insects. These can easily be despatched by spraying with a solution of either soft soap or Lux flakes – use 60g (2oz) of soap to 4.5 litres (1 gallon) of water. Alternatively, you can spray them with pyrethrum or derris. Both pyrethrum and derris are safe plant-derived pesticides that break down rapidly and so don't persist in our environment. Of the two, pyrethrum spares most beneficial insects and breaks down faster. Most garden shops should stock pyrethrum and derris, but make sure there are no other chemicals added, and follow the directions on the bottle carefully. Before spraying with an insecticide, it is a good idea to add a *small* squirt of washing up liquid to it first. This acts as a wetting agent and ensures the spray sticks to the aphids and doesn't just run off; use about a thimbleful per 4.5 litres (1 gallon) of spray.

Caterpillars

If there are just a few, the best solution is to pick them off and squash them. If there are lots of little ones, it may be quicker to use a spray. You can use derris, either on its own or mixed with an equal measure of pyrethrum. Mixing the two together in this way produces a stronger spray than if either the pyrethrum or derris were used on their own. It is however a good idea to remove any really big caterpillars by hand as these may not be killed by the spray.

Remember that even safe non-persistent pesticides like pyrethrum and derris are toxic to beneficial insects, including bees. Always try to spray in the evening when most of the friendly insects have gone home. If you must spray plants that are in bloom, use pyrethrum and always spray in the late evening when the bees have stopped foraging for the day.

Instead of using simple poisons to kill caterpillars, you can spray them with a special bacterial (*bacillus thuringiensis*) preparation. The caterpillar eats the bacteria, which start to grow in the caterpillar's gut preventing it feeding, and so it dies. This method is better than just using poison, since the bacteria are fatal only to caterpillars, and all beneficial insects are spared. This is an example of *biological control* and is a really safe and effective way of hitting only the pests without harming other creatures or putting poisons into the environment. Biological control preparations are not that widely available, so if you want to use this method to kill caterpillars, you should contact the Henry Doubleday

Research Association (see page 159) who stock this and other organic pest killers.

Slugs

A sprinkling of soot will deter slugs and snails from eating your plants. If you haven't any soot or you have a large slug or snail population in your garden, a more effective solution is Fertosan Slug Killer. This is a fine white powder which, unlike slug pellets, is only harmful to slugs and will not hurt birds and other wildlife, even if some creature happens to eat a slug or snail that has been killed by Fertosan. Some garden shops stock Fertosan, but in case of difficulty it can be bought from the Henry Doubleday Research Association – see page 159.

The best long-term solution if you are plagued by slugs and snails, is to try to reduce the number of damp places where they breed and hide during the day, but in a small garden this isn't always easy.

FURTHER READING

The following books by Lawrence Hills provide a sound introduction to organic gardening:

Organic Gardening (Penguin)
Grow Your Own Fruit and Vegetables (Faber and Faber)
A Month by Month Guide to Organic Gardening (Thorsons)

For more information on organic gardening contact:

Henry Doubleday Research Association
Ryton-on-Dunsmore
Coventry CV8 3LG

This is the largest organic gardening organization in the world and will be pleased to send you, free of charge, a comprehensive catalogue of organic gardening products and books, as well as information on the vital work being done by the Association to foster organic horticulture and agriculture.

FURTHER INFORMATION

Chapter 3
If you have difficulty getting Porosan preserving skin, write to:

Thorpac Group plc
Cirencester
Gloucestershire GL7 1LU

Mechanical sieves are available from:

Elizabeth David Ltd
46 Bourne Street
London SW1 8JD

Chapter 4
Traditional sausage cases can be bought mail order from:

Smallholding Supplies
Little Burcott
Nr Wells
Somerset BA5 1NQ

They will send you a free catalogue containing hundreds of hard-to-get items useful in the kitchen and in a self-reliant household.

Chapter 6
Freeze-dried cheese starter culture is available from:

R J Fullwood and Bland Ltd
Grange Road
Ellesmere
Shropshire SY12 9DF

Fullwood's have a free catalogue of home dairy equipment which they will send to you on request.

Chapter 7
Paté presses are available from:

Elizabeth David Ltd
46 Bourne Street
London SW1 8JD

Chapter 8
Small wooden mash tubs can be obtained from:

Earthworks
22 Corve Street
Ludlow
Shropshire

Chapter 11
If you have trouble finding Cowpost, write to:

Cowpact Ltd
Hollingdon
Leighton Buzzard
Bedfordshire LU7 0DN

Cowpost can also be obtained from:

Henry Doubleday Research Association
Ryton-on-Dunsmore
Coventry CV8 3LG

Fertosan slug killer and materials for biological control of caterpillars and other pests are also available from the same source. A catalogue detailing a huge range of organic gardening products and books is available free of charge. Nearly all of their products can be supplied mail order.

ABOUT THE AUTHOR

MIKE FOXWELL has been growing fruit and vegetables and producing food since childhood. He now runs an allotment, two small gardens, several beehives and a small dairy from his terraced house in Coventry.

He is a member of the Soil Association and the Henry Doubleday Research Association, has been Chairperson of the Heart of England Organic Groups and has had his own radio series on self-sufficiency.

Mike has been a contributor to various newspapers and magazines on self-sufficiency. This is his first book.